Return to Me

What to Do When Loved Ones Fall Away

Kathy Pollard

Gospel Advocate
Nashville, Tennessee

Published by Gospel Advocate Co.
1006 Elm Hill Pike, Nashville, TN 37210
www.gospeladvocate.com

ISBN 10: 0892256745
ISBN 13: 978-0892256747

Dedication

*For his wisdom when I floundered
when my own loved ones fell away,*

*For his patience when I needed to
talk, and talk, and talk,*

For his grace when I didn't deserve it,

For his constant support and encouragement as I wrote,

*For his willingness to be the first
to read and edit this book,*

*For his generous love,
I gratefully dedicate this book
to my husband, Neal Pollard.*

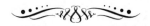

What Others Are Saying about Return to Me

"From the very first chapter, I felt that Kathy Pollard was speaking to my heart as I sensed her deep concern for those who lose their way spiritually and her desire to reach out to them in love."

—Janie Craun, editor of *Christian Woman* magazine

"The time is ripe for this topic, and Kathy broaches it with sensitivity and Godly wisdom. I highly recommend this rich resource."

—Celine Sparks, author of *What Ever Happened to Fried Chicken?*

"Kathy has managed to give sound biblical advice in a very clear and loving way. I recommend Return To Me to anyone living with this situation."

—Donna Faughn from Paducah, Kentucky

"Oh, Kathy . . . how I needed to read Return to Me, *and didn't really know I needed to read it until I read it! . . . Your gentle words truly gave me comfort, as well as the little prod I needed to proactively look for ways to catch those who may be falling through the cracks, and to love and encourage those who have already fallen."*

—Carla Moore from Dripping Springs, Texas.

Acknowledgments

Some superstars I'd like to thank:

Thank you to my sons, Gary, Dale, and Carl, for keeping me motivated by checking on my progress and then saying, "Wow, way to go!"

Thank you, Gospel Advocate, for seeing the value in this subject and wanting to get it into as many hands as possible.

Thank you, Peggy Coulter, for coming up with the perfect title.

Thank you to all those who were willing to share their experiences with me, those who have had loved ones fall away and those who have returned to the fold. May God bless each of you as you continue to encourage others and trust in God.

Thank you, Mom, for your strength as you made the difficult journey "back home," and for your example of humility and courage.

Kathy Pollard

Contents

Foreword

Occasionally a book comes along that reaches out to you in a very personal way. Reading the manuscript of *Return to Me* had that effect on me. From the very first chapter, I felt that Kathy Pollard was speaking to my heart as I sensed her deep concern for those who lose their way spiritually and her desire to reach out to them in love.

I suspect that every one of us has a close friend or loved one who once knew the Lord but has since fallen away. At one time, he or she attended the services of the church with regularity. They were involved in fellowship and other church activities. But something happened that caused them to leave the fold. Understanding why it happened and how we can bring them back results in much soul-searching on our part. We agonize, wondering how we might have contributed to their loss of faith. We pray for guidance in knowing how to approach them and what to say. We shed tears over a broken relationship. But often, that is as far as we get. In this book, Kathy has given us steps to take in initiating the process of reconciliation.

People leave the Lord for many reasons. A 2012 survey by the Pew Research Center revealed that among all religious groups in America, the ranks of the unaffiliated are swelling. This is partly true, they concluded, "because Americans who rarely go to services are more willing than in the past to drop their religious attachments altogether."[1] Other surveys show that those who leave often continue to think of themselves as Christians,

---

1 "'Nones' on the Rise," Pew Research Center, October 9, 2012, accessed April 18, 2017, http://www.pewforum.org/2012/10/09/nones-on-the-rise/.

believing they can have a relationship with the Lord that doesn't involve the church. Do your own thing: this attitude is a characteristic of today's postmodern mindset.

Within churches of Christ, we see similar trends as members come and go. Some who once were faithful in attendance and involved in the work of the local congregation begin to attend services less frequently. Cards are sent; calls are made; excuses are given. Soon they disappear altogether. When inquiries are made, we may hear, "We've been really busy" or "We've had a lot going on" or "We are attending somewhere else" (perhaps attending a community church, visiting other churches sporadically, or tuning in to a TV evangelist).

In Matthew 13, Jesus spoke to some of the reasons why people often lose their faith, and they sound familiar today. Perhaps they responded to the gospel without fully understanding the commitment that it involves. Maybe they find it too hard to deal with peer pressure from nonbelievers; or it might be that some great disappointment has touched their lives, and they have become bitter toward God or others. Sometimes, as was the case with Demas, the world just exerts a stronger pull (2 Timothy 4:10). Whatever the reason, God grieves over the unfaithful. His plea to ancient Israel, "How can I give you up?" (Hosea 11:8), is reflective of the great love He has for fallen mankind and His desire to save us from sin and eternal loss.

You will find this book compelling because the illustrations will sound familiar. You may see yourself in them along with those you love. Though not entertaining (how could reading about the errant be entertaining?), the book is written in a style that is easy to follow. It reminds us that unfaithfulness is not a new problem, as evidenced by the many Bible characters who also agonized and wept over those who left the Lord.

This book is helpful for individual use or for class study, as each chapter encourages the reader to dig through Scripture. It also includes the personal perspective of someone who is struggling to reach an errant brother, sister, parent, grandchild or personal friend. The individual shares scriptures he or she has found especially helpful along with advice about the best way to approach a similar situation.

I highly recommend this study and the one who wrote it. I believe that its unique appeal is very timely. It is my sincere hope and prayer that it will motivate and empower many of us to do a better job of "bringing the wanderer back again."

Janie Craun, editor *Christian Woman* magazine

Introduction

Return to Me

"How can I give you up, Ephraim?
How can I hand you over, Israel? ...
My heart churns within Me;
My sympathy is stirred."
Hosea 11:8

I t has to be true that the greater the love one has for another, the greater the pain when that love is rejected. A mere acquaintance who does not return overtures of friendship is no heartache. A bond forged at youth camp, which promises to keep in touch "forever and ever" but gradually fizzles out, causes no tears. But when a husband of twenty or thirty years spurns the wife of his youth in favor of a more youthful wife, the pain is unbearable. A mother whose angry son has gone the way of the world and no longer wants anything to do with her feels like her heart has been ripped from her chest.

Consider the greatest of all loves—the love God has for His children. Can we really adequately grasp the depth of God's love? Time and distance can douse friendships. Unfaithfulness can kill marriages. But nothing can separate us from the love of God (Romans 8:38, 39)! Even when the children of Israel rejected Him and repeatedly committed spiritual adultery, God pleaded, "Return to Me" (Jeremiah 3:1). God is the creator of man and the creator of love. God IS love (1 John 4:16). What immeasurable pain, then, God must experience when His children fall away!

I

Hosea's task was difficult, and his message from God was an emotional one. The faithfulness of the Israelites was described as "a morning cloud, and like the early dew it goes away" (Hosea 6:4). Hosea pleaded with the children of Israel to turn from idolatry by reminding them of the loyalty of God's love. God said He loved them from their youth, and He taught them to walk, "taking them by their arms" (11:3). He "drew them with gentle cords, with bands of love" and "stooped and fed them" (v. 4). God's tender care for His people is very apparent, and so is His hurt as He declared, "My people are bent on backsliding from Me. Though they call to the Most High, none at all exalt Him" (v. 7). None at all? To spiritually lose one child is detrimental enough. How easy, then, to understand God's grief as He cried out, "How can I give you up, Ephraim? How can I hand you over, Israel? ... My heart churns within Me; My sympathy is stirred" (v. 8).

"How can I give you up?" So many read this passage and feel their chest tighten with sympathy. They can completely relate to this question. Concerning a wayward loved one, many have thought over and over, "How can I bear to let you go?" Nothing is more painful than having a loved one fall away from the Lord. Losing someone in death is painful, but Christians can look forward to that happy reunion in heaven. Losing someone spiritually is overwhelmingly painful. In addition to the severed relationship, there is the fear of losing a loved one eternally. There is the loss of being able to pray, "Lord, come quickly," for instead there is a panic that He might return and it will be too late for the beloved prodigal.

The Father knows how we feel. He understands. We can turn to Him for guidance and help. As much as we want to wring our hands, weep, and wring our hands some more, we know that is not healthy after an extended period of time. The purpose of this book is to discuss how to cope when loved ones fall away. At the end of each chapter is a "Faith in Action" activity. Sometimes it helps just to have something tangible to do. To get the reader started, and to build a foundation for this study, there is even a suggested activity here at the end of this introduction

Also, you will find some thoughts at the end of each chapter that have been shared by individuals who have had a loved one fall away from the Lord. You are not alone. Find comfort and encouragement in their stories.

Now may the God of peace Himself sanctify you completely; and may your whole spirit, soul, and body be preserved blameless at the coming of our Lord Jesus Christ. He who calls you is faithful, who also will do it. (1 Thessalonians 5:23, 24)

∼Faith in Action∽

Go through the first several chapters of the book of Jeremiah. Underline in black (representing sin) phrases like "they have gone far from Me," "backsliding," "forsaken the Lord," "transgressed against Me," "rejected," and "My people have forgotten Me." Then underline in red (representing God's loyal love) every time God says, "return," "return to Me," or "amend your ways."

Chapter One

Keep Your Faith in God

"LET US DRAW NEAR WITH A TRUE HEART IN FULL ASSURANCE
OF FAITH ... LET US HOLD FAST THE CONFESSION OF OUR HOPE WITH-
OUT WAVERING, FOR HE WHO PROMISED IS FAITHFUL."

HEBREWS 10:22A, 23

How strong is your faith? Is it stronger than your family ties? Family is powerful. The very word draws up sentimental snapshots in the mind, such as holiday dinners, national park vacations, birthday parties, and game nights in the den. Family members have experienced both laughter and tears together. They have invested time in living together. They have created memories together. It is difficult when any loved one falls away from the Lord, but when that loved one is a family member, those precious snapshots can shatter. Spiritual backsliding from a close family member causes change and a loss of togetherness; that by itself can be a huge trial.

Sometimes our faith can be tied to a person instead of God, and we might not even be aware of it until that person falls away. A gospel preacher left his wife for another woman. For a few months the abandoned wife relied heavily on her heavenly Father. But when her husband never came back to her, anger and bitterness gradually took the place of shock and hurt. The disillusioned wife eventually turned her back on God. Her faith had been tied to her strong, Christian husband. When he let her down, she floundered. The grown children of that broken couple also struggled. They wondered how their parents, who brought them up in the church and taught them to love God and His Word, could change so completely. Was their upbringing a lie? What about those family devotionals? Were they all meaningless? They felt like their foundation had been yanked out from under them.

We must ask ourselves, "Is my faith tied to Christ?" It might be hard to really know until the time comes when my faith is put to the test. Oftentimes that trial will be in the form of a loved one falling away. If my spouse falls away, will I keep my faith in God, going to worship every week alone? If my child falls away, will I lean on the Almighty or will I blame Him? If any dear loved one falls away, what can we do to keep our faith in God?

Remember, Even Christians Have Feet of Clay

When we say someone has "feet of clay," we're referring to hidden character flaws or weaknesses not readily seen by others. The expression comes from the Bible, specifically the image in King Nebuchadnezzar's dream in Daniel 2:33. Usually the term is given to someone we admire or someone in a high position. When some discovery mars their reputation, or shatters our image of them, we say they have "feet of clay." Notice Daniel's explanation for the image's clay feet: "And as the toes of the feet were partly of iron and partly of clay, so the kingdom shall be partly strong and partly fragile" (v. 42). The clay is the weakness.

If we are not careful, disappointment in a loved one can turn into disappointment in God. We might find ourselves asking a lot of why questions. Why isn't God answering my prayers? Why do I feel like such a failure? Why do I feel all alone in this? Is God being silent for a reason? Does He even care? Our questions can have a lot to do with our expectations. It would not surprise us for a non-Christian to embrace the world and all it has to offer. But when a Christian does that, we can be caught off guard. We have expectations of those Christians we love. We expect them to be "faithful until death" (Revelation 2:10). When those expectations are not met and someone we love and trust lets us down, Satan tries to turn our disappointment into doubt. We might find ourselves struggling to trust God.

The answer is not to lower our expectations of Christians. The answer is to remember that Christians can stumble and fall. Only our Savior lived a perfect life on this earth. "For we do not have a High Priest who cannot sympathize with our weaknesses, but was in all points tempted as we are, yet without sin" (Hebrews 4:15). Aside from Jesus, not a single person, past or present, can claim to be sinless. Unfortunately, sometimes a dear brother or sister will stumble and fall, and not get back up.

Satan is after the very strongest of Christians! Notice how active the Scriptures portray the devil.

» He **lies** (John 8:44).
» He **tempts** married couples (1 Corinthians 7:5).
» He **takes advantage** of us by using devices (2 Corinthians 2:11).
» He **blinds** us to the truth (2 Corinthians 4:4).
» He **disguises** himself as an angel of light (2 Corinthians 11:14).
» He **hinders** the work of the church (1 Thessalonians 2:18).
» He **walks** about as a roaring lion, **seeking** someone to devour (1 Peter 5:8).
» He **deceives** the whole world (Revelation 12:9).

In fact, Paul said we "*wrestle* ... against the rulers of the darkness of this age" and we have to *shield* ourselves from the "fiery darts of the wicked one" (Ephesians 6:12, 16). The devil is real, and he is mission-minded. His mission is to turn faithful Christians away from God. He wants to attack the church. He wants to destroy our families. And he will use whatever means it takes to accomplish his mission. The devil is so aptly named in Revelation 9:11:

And they had as king over them the angel of the bottomless pit, whose name in Hebrew is Abaddon, but in Greek he has the name Apollyon.

Abaddon literally means "Destruction," and *Apollyon* literally means "Destroyer." Satan is actively trying to ruin the lives of faithful Christians.

Paul reminded us that even though one may be in the best spiritual environment, one can still give in to temptation. The children of God had experienced the miraculous passing through the Red Sea, eaten spiritual food, quenched their thirst with spiritual drink, and had the Rock of Christ, and yet, "with most of them God was not well pleased" (1 Corinthians 10:5). Though they had obvious and visible signs of God being with them, they still committed idolatry and sexual immorality. They still tried the Lord and murmured. Paul called them examples for us, and so he warned, "Therefore let him who thinks he stands take heed lest he fall" (v. 12).

David, the man after God's own heart, committed adultery and murder. Judas, one who actually walked with Jesus as one of His apostles, allowed Satan to enter his heart (John 13:27). Demas went from follower to forsaker (Colossians 4:14; 2 Timothy 4:10). No matter how great, how strong, or how spiritual someone is they still battle temptation. No one is infallible. When Job struggled after losing everything, he asked God to remember that he was made of clay (Job 10:9).

Remember God's Faithful Love

When disappointed by a loved one, it's all too easy to blame God or develop a skewed picture of God. Severe pain and suffering cause some to want nothing to do with God. For instance, there are some Christian parents of the Columbine victims who are no longer faithful. The tragedy was too great. Instead of turning to God, they turned away from Him. They are angry with God and feel He has let them down.

Have you noticed how no one is surprised when something like that happens? I heard someone talking about a couple that had once been very active in the Lord's church, but now they want nothing to do with religion. When I asked why, the answer was given, "They lost a son in the Columbine shooting." I just replied, "Oh, I see." And we do see. We may have experienced the temptation ourselves, the temptation to walk away from God when overwhelmed with pain. Even though we know it's not right to blame God, we understand how it could happen. Hurt and confusion, hard times, or disappointment can cloud one's vision of God's abiding love.

Having a loved one fall away is surely one of the most painful things we can experience in this life. The ache saturates different levels—physical, emotional, mental, and spiritual—and, if not dealt with properly, can cause us to lash out in all the wrong ways and places. So how can we remember God's faithful love during such a difficult time?

Don't transfer feelings of anger, resentment, and disappointment.

There is a certain measure of anger toward those who have fallen away. We wonder how they could be so selfish as to hurt their family. We may even resent them for causing the turmoil and pain. And certainly there is great disappointment. What happened to their faith? Wasn't their relationship with God real? After the feelings of anger and disappointment are expressed, we might not get the reaction we desired. We might not get a reaction at all, in fact, if the wayward one has reached the point of emotional disconnect. Sometimes, then, those feelings still need an outlet. But instead of expressing them to God, in order to release their burdens to Him, some develop those feelings toward God. They transfer all of their negative feelings and begin to blame God for all that happened. But God's not the one who left. He didn't walk away, disappoint, or stop loving, and He never will.

Don't bring God down to man's level.

Christians make mistakes. We hurt people, intentionally or unintentionally. We let people down. God never does. So when someone is angry with God, they need to stop and ask themselves why. Jonah became angry with God when He didn't strike down the Ninevites. Jonah's heart longed for vengeance, and he didn't think God was being fair. But God is gracious and compassionate, and He is always fair (Jonah 3:10–4:11). Jonah was wrong about God. When Martha was angry with Mary, she took her frustrations out on Jesus. She said, "Lord, do You not care that my sister has left me to serve alone? Therefore tell her to help me" (Luke 10:40). Did you catch that? Martha knew Jesus was the Son of God, but she still accused Him of not caring. She drew that conclusion when Jesus didn't do what she expected of Him. Of course Jesus cared! He cared so much that He wanted what was best for both Mary and Martha (vv. 41, 42). Martha was wrong about Jesus. If we become angry with God, we need to ask ourselves why. Do we think He doesn't care? Do we think He should've acted on our behalf or in our favor? God is all knowing and all seeing (1 John 3:20). He doesn't think like we think (Isaiah 55:8, 9). To be angry with Him is to bring Him down to man's level, to assume that we know what's best.

Do reacquaint yourself with the nature of God's love.

God's love is nothing like man's imperfect love. God's love is perfect and everlasting. When things are going well, we are secure in that knowledge. But sometimes, especially when our hearts are hurting, we forget the amazing depth and enduring nature of God's love. Could it be Satan whispers doubts in our minds about God's love? Like Mrs. Job advising her husband to "curse God and die" (Job 2:9), Satan's lies begin with God to get us to turn away from Him. When he tempted Eve, Satan mentioned God's name three times (Genesis 3:1–5). To keep ourselves from ever believing Satan's lies about God, we need to continually reacquaint ourselves with the love of God. The Word is filled with the truth about God's love. Study it often so its voice will be louder than Satan's.

Do anchor your soul in the knowledge of God's promises.

Our hope is secure in the fact that we are heirs of God's promise and God keeps His promises. This hope is our "anchor of the soul" (Hebrews 6:19). How reliable is that anchor when we are assailed by the storms of life? The Bible describes it as "sure and steadfast." The word "sure" means it is certain, solid, and reliable.[1] "Steadfast" means it stands firm on the feet and doesn't break down under what steps upon it.[2] No matter what

---

1 G. Friedrich, G. Kittel, and G.W. Bromily, eds., *Theological Dictionary of the New Testament* (Grand Rapids: Eerdmans, 1995), 87.

2 G. Friedrich, G. Kittel, and G.W. Bromily, eds., *Theological Dictionary of the New Testament*, electronic ed. (Grand Rapids: Eerdmans, 1964).

burdens press, our feet won't be knocked out from under us. No matter what winds of turmoil beat at us, we can weather them if our faith is anchored in God.

Does Jesus Care?

By Frank E. Graeff

Does Jesus care when my heart is pained
too deeply for mirth or song,
as the burdens press, and the cares distress,
and the way grows weary and long?

Does Jesus care when my way is dark
with a nameless dread and fear?
As the daylight fades into deep night shades,
does He care enough to be near?

Does Jesus care when I've tried and failed
to resist some temptation strong;
when for my deep grief there is no relief,
though my tears flow all the night long?

Does Jesus care when I've said "goodbye"
to the dearest on earth to me,
and my sad heart aches till it nearly breaks—
is it aught to Him? Does He see?

Oh, yes, He cares, I know He cares,
His heart is touched with my grief;
when the days are weary, the long nights dreary,
I know my Savior cares.

∾Faith in Action∾

Consider the beloved song "Does Jesus Care?" Find an example in the Bible of someone experiencing the particular kind of suffering mentioned in each verse of the song (pain, fear, temptation, loss, etc.). How did God show His care in each situation? Now think of someone you know who is suffering. Send them a card reminding them that God cares. Include a couple of encouraging scriptures.

Apply Your Heart (Proverbs 2:2)

Martin Luther King Jr. said, "There can be no deep disappointment where there is not deep love." Have you been disappointed by someone close to you? If so, did you react positively (praying, meditating on the Word, talking through it)? Or did you react in ways you regret (blaming, looking for ways to hurt back)? What did you learn that will help you if it ever happens again?

Is Danger Nearby?
     Examine each of the close relationships in your life. Are any of them dangerously close to replacing Christ as your anchor?

Fortify Your Faith
     List one word next to each verse that describes the nature of God's love:

Jeremiah 31:3   _____

John 3:16   _____

Romans 5:8   _____

Ephesians 2:4   _____

2 Thessalonians 2:16, 17   _____

A Wife's Perspective

HER STORY: "My husband left me and the church. He has been unfaithful for fourteen years."

SCRIPTURES SHE'S RELIED ON: 2 Corinthians 1:3–11; 4:7, 8, 16–18; Psalm 13; 23; 119:49, 50, 75, 76; Romans 8:28–39; Ephesians 1:3–10; Philippians 4:4–8; Colossians 3:12, 13; 1 John 5:13, 14; Isaiah 40:28–31; 46:3, 4

ADVICE SHE'D OFFER TO SOMEONE IN A SIMILAR SITUATION: "First, don't let that person's unfaithfulness become a weight that drags you down. Satan is looking for anything he can find to catch you in his snare. God, on the other hand, is ready to lift you up. Second, don't blame yourself for their unfaithfulness. As with anything, there probably were things you could've done better or differently, but ultimately it was their decision to leave God."

ADDITIONAL THOUGHTS: "Even now, 14 years later, I still hurt for [my husband] and the decision he made to leave God. If I feel this badly, how much greater is God's hurt? After all, God allowed His Son to die, and [my husband] rejected that sacrifice. But I haven't given up on him. I still hope [and] pray … that he will return to God."

Chapter Two

Guard Your Own Soul

"PONDER THE PATH OF YOUR FEET, AND
LET ALL YOUR WAYS BE ESTABLISHED."

PROVERBS 4:26

When a loved one falls away, you might feel wounded, as if you've been stabbed. You might feel down, as if your feet have been knocked out from under you. In other words, you feel vulnerable.

According to Merriam-Webster.com, *vulnerable* means "capable of being physically or emotionally wounded; open to attack or damage." Have you felt any of those things? Vulnerability can be dangerous.

Those who've had a loved one fall away, and then eventually fell away themselves, were once vulnerable. Because vulnerability is a frightening and unsettling feeling, they chose to protect themselves, but they did it the wrong way. Perhaps they protected themselves by cutting off all feeling. Their new mantra became "I don't care anymore." Perhaps they protected themselves by acting out in rebellion. They engaged in willful sin to prove a point: "Now you know how it feels!" Or perhaps they protected themselves by becoming hard. They determined never to love again, never to be open to the possibility of pain. They walled themselves up and became unapproachable, closed off.

The Dangers of Vulnerability

When one is vulnerable, there are many dangerous feelings that, if not handled the right way, can lead to spiritual decline.

Disappointment

Disappointment is a natural part of this earthly life. Normally we're aware of that fact and can handle it with grace, looking forward to the day when we'll never be disappointed again. As the old song says, "There's no disappointment in heaven!"

However, when we're vulnerable, the disappointment can seem like too much. We start assuming that others will disappoint us as well—our closest friends, our family members, our Christian brothers and sisters, and even the elders. This assumption leads to distrust and suspicion, which are unhealthy for any relationship.

Anger

Righteous indignation and anger may play a large part in your reaction to a loved one falling away. But oh, how many times have we sinned ourselves in our anger over some injustice or deception? Anger is such a powerfully strong emotion. It fuels. It grows. It boils. The popular saying sums it up well: "Anger is only one letter short of danger." When angry, it's too easy to lash out or say hurtful things that can never be recalled (or forgotten). The Bible warns, "'Be angry, and do not sin': do not let the sun go down on your wrath, nor give place to the devil" (Ephesians 4:26, 27). When anger is present, Satan hovers.

Discouragement

After repeated, failed attempts to persuade a loved one to return to the Lord, the discouragement can be overwhelming. Discouragement can cause us to make rash decisions. It can make us question our capabilities. Ultimately, the smothering darkness of discouragement can snuff out all hope, and so we give up. "I'm just so tired of it all." "I can't take anymore." "I quit."

Bitterness

Grudge-bearing, difficulty forgiving, unresolved anger: these can lead to the unpalatable root of bitterness. Even a little bitterness in the heart will manifest itself in acrid speech. It's hard to hide. Like an invasive weed, bitterness spreads quickly and takes diligent effort to uproot. No wonder God commands us to put all bitterness away from us (Ephesians 4:31).

Guard Your Soul with Faith

So how can we guard our souls against these natural but dangerous feelings? When disappointment or discouragement becomes a constant companion, how can we keep our own selves from blaming God or falling away? The only answer is that we must fortify our faith.

Romans 5:1–5 is a power-packed passage that reminds us of the beautiful significance of faith:

> *Therefore, having been justified by faith, we have peace with God through our Lord Jesus Christ, through whom also we have access by faith into this grace in which we stand, and rejoice in hope of the glory of God. And not only that, but we also glory in tribulations, knowing that tribulation produces perseverance; and perseverance, character; and character, hope. Now hope does not disappoint, because the love of God has been poured out in our hearts by the Holy Spirit who was given to us.*

Notice what we can claim because of faith:

We have "peace with God" (v. 1).

When discouraged and heartsick, our relationship with God may suffer. We may question God's love for us or doubt He's really in control. A fortified faith keeps us confident in God's presence. In context, peace with God was made possible by the blood of Christ. His sacrifice removed the separation of sin and repaired a severed relationship. When God seems far, a fortified faith brings Him near. Peace with God means no more doubt, no more anger, and no more separation.

We can "stand in grace" (v. 2).

The ability to stand takes on a whole new appreciation when it feels as if your feet have been knocked out from under you. A closer look at the Greek word for "stand" here reveals an even deeper meaning. According to the *Theological Dictionary of the New Testament*, "it involves the place where a person is set or stands and the question of what endures in the flux of time with its changes."[1] In other words, we can stand firm, no matter what shakes our foundation. We can remain in the faith!

We can "rejoice in hope" (v. 2).

This is the lifeline we cling to when dark days make it hard to see any happy outcome. We have hope! For that reason alone, we can give ourselves permission to rejoice, even when someone we love has turned away from that hope. We'll discuss hope a little more when we get to verse 5.

We can "glory in tribulations" (v. 3).

Tribulation is "trouble involving direct suffering."[2] According to our text, the reason we can glory in tribulation is because of what it produces—perseverance, character, and hope (vv. 3, 4). These are three supremely good things that come from remaining faithful during trials. Perseverance is the ability to endure difficulties, no matter how long they last. Character is the refining we gain from persevering. We've been tested in battle and found reliable. And hope is realized by those with the character that comes from persevering. Do you see how they are progressive, steadily stepping toward a better condition? A fortified faith allows us to see the benefits of enduring trials. "My brethren, count it all joy when you fall into various trials, knowing that the testing of your faith produces patience. But let patience have its perfect work, that you may be perfect and complete, lacking nothing" (James 1:2–4).

So far we've seen from these verses that faith gives us peace, stability,

---

1 G. Kittel, G. Friedrich, and G.W. Bromily, eds., *Theological Dictionary of the New Testament*, electronic ed. (Grand Rapids: Eerdmans, 1964).

2 J. Louw and E.A. Nida, *Greek-English Lexicon of the New Testament: Based on Semantic Domains*. electronic ed. of 2nd ed. (New York: United Bible Societes, 1996).

hope, and growth. The final verse in our text ends on another wonderfully bright note about hope: "Hope does not disappoint" (Romans 5:5). Hope is what pushes weary soldiers to keep fighting the battle. Hope is what keeps a young couple from closing the door on their marriage when strife knocks. The word "hope" is mentioned a total of three times in Romans 5:1–5. We have a hope because of God's glory (v. 2), a hope that comes from tribulation (vv. 3, 4), and a hope that does not disappoint (v. 5). It is a hope that is true, faithful, and dependable! Why? Because of God's love in our hearts (v. 5). How much love? Some love? A little? No, bountiful love. God's love was poured out in our hearts. God's love will never betray us or disappoint us. People may let us down, but God never will. It is this hope—built on a fortified faith and sealed by the love of God—that will keep us strong when we feel so weak. As Mignon McLaughlin said, "Hope is the feeling we have that the feeling we have is not permanent."

My husband, Neal, came up with a list that I found so helpful I made copies and displayed them on my refrigerator, the wall behind my ironing board, and my sons' bathroom wall. Since this chapter discusses the need to guard our own souls, it seemed appropriate to share Neal's list with you (see page 21).

⟿Faith in Action⟿

Memorize Romans 5:1–5. The ability to recall this passage at any time will be a spiritual boost when disappointments come. You might even challenge a few friends to memorize it with you (Ecclesiastes 4:9–12).

Apply Your Heart (Proverbs 2:2)

Strengthen Yourself in the Lord

Read the tragic incident recorded in 1 Samuel 30:1–6. David and his men discovered their city burned and their women taken captive by the enemy. The people "wept, until they had no more power to weep." David was "greatly distressed." The very "soul" of the people was "grieved." In this text, we have two different reactions to the same sad discovery. The people, in their grief and fear, reacted by wanting to lash out and hurt someone. They wanted to make someone pay. This reaction led to sin because they targeted David and went so far as to discuss stoning him. Their feelings were legitimate, but how they handled them was dangerous. "But David strengthened himself in the LORD his God" (v. 6). The people reacted by looking around for someone to blame. David reacted by looking up to his God. He went to the priest, and he "inquired of the LORD" (vv. 7, 8). When faced with an unhappy turn of events, what are some specific ways you can strengthen yourself in the Lord?

Why Call Upon the Lord

In Psalm 55, David wrote about being hurt and betrayed by someone he cared about (see vv. 12–14). List the ways he described his feelings to God throughout this psalm. What reasons did David give for calling upon God (see vv. 16–19, 22)?

Fortify Your Faith

Think of ways to fortify your faith on a continual basis so that you can guard your own soul when deeply disappointed by those you love.

25 Ways to Keep Christ in the Center of My Life

By Neal Pollard

1. I will absorb myself in the practice of prayer.
2. I will actively practice kindness.
3. I will find someone each day with whom to share Him.
4. I will watch what I allow to grow in my heart.
5. I will consider carefully how what I do affects my influence.
6. I will actively encourage the people I daily encounter.
7. I will assume and look for the best in others.
8. I will nurture a hatred of sin and a love of sinners.
9. I will treat Scripture as a daily nourishment for my soul.
10. I will keep a spiritual song in my heart.
11. I will reflect meaningfully on the price He paid at Calvary.
12. I will guard my tongue.
13. I will think longingly about heaven.
14. I will contemplate ways to be involved in the church's work.
15. I will love His church with a passion (that means the people, too).
16. I will cut out the tendency to rationalize or defend wrongdoing.
17. I will be discerning about what is spiritual and what is worldly.
18. I will grow in my understanding of what true love is.
19. I will humbly acknowledge the greatness and power of God.
20. I will do all within my power to help answer His prayer for unity.
21. I will pursue souls with the same vigor that He did.
22. I will look for ways to turn the conversation to the spiritual.
23. I will long for times of worship and devotion.
24. I will care less and less about my rights, feelings, and desires.
25. I will think, speak, act, and look more like Him every day.

A Daughter's Perspective

HER STORY: "After years of teaching others the truth and preaching the gospel, my father left the Lord after committing adultery and leaving my mother. He has been unfaithful for the past ten years."

SCRIPTURES SHE'S RELIED ON: Romans 8:28; Psalm 46:1, 2; Mark 11:24; Philippians 4:6, 7

ADVICE SHE'D OFFER TO SOMEONE IN A SIMILAR SITUATION: "It can shatter your faith. Blame sin, not God. Get past the hurt and anger—see the soul."

ADDITIONAL THOUGHTS: "Never take your marriage for granted. Never think it can never happen to you. And never give up on them!"

Chapter Three

Lean on God's Family

"AND IF ONE MEMBER SUFFERS, ALL THE MEMBERS SUFFER
WITH IT; OR IF ONE MEMBER IS HONORED,
ALL THE MEMBERS REJOICE WITH IT."
1 CORINTHIANS 12:26

Thank God for His family, the church. Our Christian family is a precious gift, and no more so than when our relationships with other dear ones have suffered or been severed. Lean on God's family for support. When we're physically exhausted, we lean against the wall so we can remain upright. When we're physically impaired, we lean against a cane or walker so we can get where we need to go. When those times of spiritual exhaustion or impairment come, how wonderful that we can lean on God's family to help us remain upright and get where we need to go!

When a loved one falls away from the Lord, we must conjure up every bit of strength we have to do what needs to be done. It's not easy, and we may wonder at times how long we have to continue being so strong. Our church family can help ease the burden. Their strength helps lighten the load so we can carry on. Think how much easier it is to stick to a strict diet when your spouse agrees to diet with you. Or how much quicker an hour on the treadmill goes by when there's a friend on the one next to you. Diet and exercise are hard things that require diligence and discipline, but they're made a little easier when we're not doing them alone.

Members of God's Family

Our brothers and sisters in Christ make it easier for us to run the race faithfully unto death (Revelation 2:10). They pull us along when we think we can't take the next step. Consider some of the members that are found in God's family:

Sister Been There, Done That

She has been through the same thing. The details may be different, but the story's the same. She has suffered the heartache of having a loved one fall away from God. She understands your pain, fear, and anger. She can sympathize with your struggles. You wonder why you can't stop crying, but she gets it. And, really, there are probably lots of members in your local church family who have experienced losing someone to the world.

Brother Faithful

He has been through so much. Perhaps he has had more than one loved one fall away from God, but he is still faithful. Despite the disappointments and broken hearts, his trust in his Father is complete and evident. His example of steadfastness is a reminder that we can do all things with the strength of Christ (Philippians 4:13).

Sister Wise

She has learned much from the trials that came her way (James 1:2–5). She can be counted on to give advice that's sound and biblical. Her years of experience and study have taught her to see earthly things through heavenly eyes.

Brother Tough Love

He knows what it's like to face dear ones and tell them he can't be with them because he can't condone what they're doing. He has heard the same accusations from those who have fallen away. "You don't understand agape love." "You are judgmental." "You think you're so perfect." And yet he has held fast to his convictions and not given in to sentiment or caved for the sake of family peace. If you ever wonder if you're being too hard, he can remind you that God's way is always the best way.

Sister Positive

She is a bright spot in the midst of dark times. Her reliable cheerfulness can be just the boost needed to face another day. She exemplifies serenity and peace when sailing troubled waters. When everyone else is shaking their heads, she can offer a positive word of encouragement.

Brother Compassionate

He can be counted on to offer unconditional love and comfort. While you struggle with feelings of responsibility or accountability, he is quick to give you a warm hug and sincere smile. He knows things haven't gone well. He knows you may have said some things you regret. He even knows you may be struggling in your own relationship with God, but he is loving anyway. His care and sympathy can be as essential as air when feeling discouraged.

Sister Listening Ear

She understands that the need to talk can be long term. She doesn't roll her eyes when you need to hash it out again. She is always willing to listen patiently, knowing what a tremendous relief that can be for someone who is six months or even six years into a painful situation.

This list of members doesn't even include the elders, who are tasked with shepherding the flock. They care about souls. We can ask them to pray for us and for our loved ones who have wandered. And what about those dear elders' wives? They've had to learn to be tough, yet tender. They can keep a confidence. Oh, how God blessed us when He structured His church! May He richly bless all elders and their wives as they serve such a crucial role in His flock.

How to Cope When You Realize God's Family Isn't Perfect

Even though the spiritual family is a blessing from God, some choose not to take advantage of this resource. Some feel more comfortable talking to a stranger than sharing their burdens with their church family. Perhaps they used to rely on God's family, but then someone said or did something that let them down. Since the church is made up of humans, we must understand how possible it is for that to happen. But instead of giving up or refusing to trust in our brethren, we should learn how to cope when we don't get the response we expect. When members say something hurtful:

Remember their good intentions.

Most often, they have no idea they just said something insensitive. Their intent is to comfort or to show that they understand. They may try to compare your situation to theirs, and you don't want them to. They may say something discouraging like "My father fell away, too, and he never came back." That's not what you need to hear, but they were just trying to show you that they understand your pain. Be grateful for their willingness to reach out to you.

Remember they're human.

The church is made up of weak, imperfect Christians. We don't always know the right thing to say or have the wisdom needed for every circumstance. Some might take scriptures out of context when trying to teach you how to handle a delicate situation. Some might slip up and share your confidences with someone else. Some might offer unsolicited advice. It could be because they just want to "fix" everything. Or, frankly, it could be because they're busybodies. It happens.

Let's offer the same patience and forgiveness to others that we desire for ourselves. Pray about it. Learn whom you can trust with your secrets. Don't give up on your church family. They won't give up on you.

Determine if it was something you needed to hear.

It could be that they are practicing tough love on YOU. Maybe you really are mishandling a situation or neglecting to follow what the Scriptures instruct. Perhaps you need teaching and admonishing. That can hurt, but it's necessary and it's a demonstration of the love your brothers and sisters in Christ have for you.

There's an old story about a preacher who visited one of the members who had been missing worship services. The member defended his lack of attendance by saying, "I believe I can be just as good a Christian outside the church as I can be inside it." Instead of replying, the preacher removed one burning coal from the fireplace and set it on the hearth. The two men watched as the ember slowly died out. "I see," the member said. What better visual to illustrate the importance of being with God's family? Satan doesn't want us to lean on our brothers and sisters. He wants our fire to burn out. We need the support of other Christians in order to keep serving, teaching, evangelizing, helping, loving, and shining.

⌁Faith in Action⌁

On a sheet of paper, list the members that were mentioned in this chapter (including the elders and their wives). Next to each one, write down the name of a specific person you know in the Lord's church who fits the characteristic or role (faithful, cheerful, etc.). First, say a prayer thanking God for putting each of the individuals in your life. Second, personally thank each one of them for what they mean to you and for the example they've set.

Apply Your Heart (Proverbs 2:2)

1. Think about God's family and read Romans 12. Every time you come across instruction on how we are to treat each other, write it down. Circle the ones in which you need to improve.

2. This lesson focused on the fact that we should lean on our brothers and sisters in Christ. We also should make sure our brothers and sisters feel they can lean on us. What are some ways you can be more aware of the needs of others? How can you reach out and let them know you'd like to help? And what kind of member are you? Are you wise, cheerful, faithful, compassionate, or positive?

3. Use a dictionary and write down the definitions of the words "encourage," "admonish," and "exhort." Find a scripture for each one that teaches how we are to do those things.

A Sister's Perspective

HER STORY: "My sister and her family left the Lord seven years ago."

SCRIPTURES SHE'S RELIED ON: 2 Peter 2:9; Proverbs 22:6

ADVICE SHE'D OFFER TO SOMEONE IN A SIMILAR SITUATION: "Our tendency, especially as women, is to 'fix it (or kiss it) and make it better.' In these kinds of situations, we must turn it over to God. But 'turning it over' requires lots of prayer AND study. We need to cocoon ourselves in God's Word and God's people. That way we are filled with the peace and love that only God can supply, but we are also equipped with God's Word to be prepared when our loved ones reach out."

Chapter Four

Seek Guidance from God's Word

"AND THAT FROM CHILDHOOD
YOU HAVE KNOWN THE HOLY SCRIPTURES,
WHICH ARE ABLE TO MAKE YOU WISE FOR SALVATION
THROUGH FAITH WHICH IS IN CHRIST JESUS."
2 TIMOTHY 3:15

According to 1 Kings 10, the Queen of Sheba was a seeker. When she heard of the famous Solomon and the wisdom God gave him, she took action. She went on a long, tedious journey in order to increase her knowledge. She mentally prepared by thinking of hard questions to ask Solomon (v. 1). She spoke with Solomon about all that was on her heart (v. 2). "Solomon answered all her questions; there was nothing so difficult for the king that he could not explain it to her" (v. 3). So the Queen of Sheba was in awe of his wisdom (vv. 4, 5). She recognized the value of his wisdom and knew that it brought happiness to those who continually heard it (v. 8). As a result, she praised God (v. 9). She knew her journey was rewarded, and she acknowledged God's hand in it. I can only imagine that the Queen of Sheba was never the same after her encounter with Solomon.

The Queen of Sheba went to an earthly king. We can go to the King of Kings! We can take our hard questions to the source of great wisdom (Proverbs 1:1–7; 2:1–6).

He wants us to pour out our hearts to Him (Proverbs 3:5, 6). We should approach the Word with awe, recognize its value, and understand that happiness only comes to those who follow the guidelines therein (vv. 13–18). How many times have we seen loved ones bring misery on themselves when they rejected God's Word?

When Jesus spoke of the queen's willingness to travel to Jerusalem, He said, "Something greater than Solomon is here" (Matthew 12:42 ESV). He was referring to the gospel. It is much greater than all of Solomon's wisdom. Do we recognize its value? When we seek wisdom and find it, we should give God the glory. We should praise His name for loving us enough to instruct us and give us guidance. The Queen of Sheba was generous with material gifts and praise. Too often, we seek and ask but neglect to give and thank. Praise God for His excellent greatness (Psalm 150)!

Why God's Word?
It's perfect.

> All Scripture is given by inspiration of God, and is profitable for doctrine, for reproof, for correction, for instruction in righteousness, that the man of God may be complete, thoroughly equipped for every good work (2 Timothy 3:16, 17).

It's perfect because every word in the Bible came from God. That means there are no errors or contradictions. There are no premature claims that time has proven false. Nothing has ever been retracted. Why? It is God-breathed, and "His work is perfect" (Deuteronomy 32:3, 4).

The Word is perfect because it provides everything we need. It's "profitable" (useful, advantageous) for four things:

DOCTRINE—This word refers to teaching. When being schooled by the trials of life, the Word needs to be our teacher. There is much we can learn! To survive (and even thrive), we must meditate in the law of the Lord day and night (Psalm 1:1–3).

REPROOF—This word means convincing, refuting, and investigating. This is for our protection. Sometimes it's hard to know what to believe, what to do, where to turn. We must make sure the truth is what's convincing us, not our emotions. Investigate the Word. It will never lead us astray (Ephesians 4:14, 15).

CORRECTION—This word means improvement, straightening, setting right. Powerful feelings are involved when a loved one falls away. We can be blindly led by them without realizing we're placing our feelings over God's will. This one can be painful (Hebrews 12:11), but do we want to be crooked in our thinking? The Word can set us straight. "Stand perfect and complete in all the will of God" (Colossians 4:12).

INSTRUCTION IN RIGHTEOUSNESS—This refers to education and training in the things that are right. God is righteous and just (Psalm 71:15, 16). He doesn't think like we do (Isaiah 55:8, 9). We need to be trained in what God says is right instead of swallowing what others or we *think* is right.

It's powerful.

For the word of God is living and powerful, and sharper than any two-edged sword, piercing even to the division of soul and spirit, and of joints and marrow, and is a discerner of the thoughts and intents of the heart. (Hebrews 4:12)

What a gift God has given us! Our Bibles are living, powerful, sharp, piercing, and discerning. Don't we need all of those things when a loved one falls away? We have something living, not dead. We have something more powerful than anything the world can offer. We have something that pierces our very being. It cuts through to the heart of the matter. We have something that discerns hidden thoughts and motives.

When emotionally drained, we may feel numb or at loose ends. We may get to the point where we can barely hang on to our Christian walk. Or we may find ourselves just going through the motions. The verse before warns us to "be diligent ... lest anyone fall according to the same example of disobedience" (Hebrews 4:11). Remember to let the Word do its powerful work!

It's productive.

Look closely at 2 Peter 1:3–8:

> *As His divine power has given to us all things that pertain to life and godliness, through the knowledge of Him who called us by glory and virtue, by which have been given to us exceedingly great and precious promises, that through these you may be partakers of the divine nature, having escaped the corruption that is in the world through lust. But also for this very reason, giving all diligence, add to your faith virtue, to virtue knowledge, to knowledge self-control, to self-control perseverance, to perseverance godliness, to godliness brotherly kindness, and to brotherly kindness love. For if these things are yours and abound, you will be neither barren nor unfruitful in the knowledge of our Lord Jesus Christ.*

In these few short verses, the word "knowledge" is used four times. (If you like, circle them to make it easier to see what we're about to discover.) Peter used two slightly different words for "knowledge." In verses 5 and 6, the word is *gnosis* and means "the intelligent comprehension of an object or matter, whether this comes for the first time, or comes afresh, into the consideration of the one who grasps it."[1]

The Word is productive because it helps us keep learning, thereby continuing to grow in our Christian walk. The word for "knowledge" used in verses 3 and 8 is *epignosis*. It is "more intensive than *gnosis* because it expresses a more thorough participation in the acquiring of knowledge on the part of the learner. In the New Testament, it often refers to knowledge which very powerfully influences the form of religious life, a knowledge laying claim to personal involvement."[2] This knowledge is more than just learning. It's a knowledge gained from experiencing God's truths and growing in one's confidence of the benefits of living God's way. The two types of knowledge could almost be simplified to "Bible-learning"

---

1 G. Kittel, G. Friedrich, and G.W. Bromily, eds., *Theological Dictionary of the New Testament*, electronic ed. (Grand Rapids: Eerdmans, 1964).

2 S. Zodhiates, *The Complete Word Study Dictionary: New Testament*, electronic ed. (Chatanooga: AMG Publishers, 2000).

and "Bible-experiencing." One leads to the other. Peter said if we grow in Bible knowledge, we will be fruitful in (experiential) knowledge of Jesus Christ. That's why we want to seek guidance from God's Word!

When to Seek God's Word

The obvious answer is "all the time." The Bible is our daily bread, our sustenance. We are to meditate on it if we want to flourish (Joshua 1:8; Psalm 1). But for the sake of this study, let's look at specific times when seeking guidance from God's Word is crucial.

When Feeling Emotional

Emotions, both positive and negative, are powerful, and certainly our emotions are involved when a loved one falls away. Our society places an emphasis on letting personal emotions guide important decisions. "I have to follow my heart." "Do what feels right to you." The world's mantra is that, while rules are good, ultimately people should live by what feels right to them.

But feelings can be an unreliable and unsafe guide. What "seems right" to us could result in disaster (Proverbs 14:12). "The heart is deceitful above all things" (Jeremiah 17:9). When Saul persecuted Christians, he wasn't trying to be wicked. He thought he was doing the right thing. He was following his heart. He didn't realize his actions were contrary to God's will. He said, "Indeed, I myself thought ..." (Acts 26:9). He was convicted by his feelings. His conscience never once made him question his actions (23:1). Even good people make huge mistakes when allowing their feelings to guide them. It wasn't until Saul encountered Christ that he learned to "speak the words of truth and reason" (26:25).

Wise Solomon summed it all up by saying, "He who trusts in his own heart is a fool" (Proverbs 28:26). When a loved one falls away, we must be aware of the danger of being led by our feelings. It can happen without us even realizing it. The way to safeguard against this is to stay in the Word. "Let my heart be blameless regarding Your statutes, that I may not be ashamed" (Psalm 119:80). Elisabeth Elliot said, "Obedience to God is

always possible. It is a deadly error to fall into the notion that when feelings are extremely strong we can do nothing but act on them."

Another reason to seek guidance from the Bible when emotional is
because our feelings can blind us to the truth and, as a result, can lead
to discouragement. The Word can help us discern between feelings
and truth.

Consider some common feelings when a loved one has fallen away
(see chart).

FEELING	TRUTH
"It's hopeless."	God reigns—Romans 8:28
"I can't do this."	God can—2 Corinthians 12:8–10
"He/She hurt me."	They're captive—Ephesians 6:12
"I'm all alone."	Never!—Hebrews 13:5, 6

When You Think You Have All the Answers

You've probably heard that women are "fixers" by nature. When there's
a problem, we want to fix it. When someone's heart is broken, we want
to mend it. And when someone falls away, we may feel the need to tell
them exactly what they need to do to get back on track. This is a good
and loving thing to do, as long as what we're telling them is in line with
God's Word.

It would be dangerous indeed to begin counseling or offering advice
without first consulting God's Word. It doesn't matter how long we've
been in the church. Why? First, souls are at stake. We would never want
to be responsible for offering any advice that actually goes against God's
will. Even if we think we already know how a situation should be handled, it would be wise to look up book, chapter, and verse to share with
the person we're trying to help. Second, others could be watching. Some-

one may be dealing privately with a similar situation and wondering how to handle it. The counsel we offer to a loved one could be adopted by someone else, without our ever being aware of it. The actions we take could set a precedent for others, whether it was the best course or not. We could call it "responsible influence," that is, making sure everything we say and do is based on God's Word. And finally, we need to seek God's Word even when we think we already know the answers because God's thoughts are superior to ours. "'For My thoughts are not your thoughts, nor are your ways My ways,' says the LORD. 'For as the heavens are higher than the earth, so are My ways higher than your ways, and My thoughts than your thoughts'" (Isaiah 55:8, 9). His Word is mistake-free. His advice is always right. The more Scripture comes out of our mouths, the more we can be confident we're leading someone in the right direction.

In our rush to help someone, here are some scriptures to remind us to take time to seek God's guidance first:

"The humble He guides in justice, and the humble He teaches His way" (Psalm 25:9).

"For the LORD gives wisdom; from His mouth come knowledge and understanding; He stores up sound wisdom for the upright; He is a shield to those who walk uprightly; ... Then you will understand righteousness and justice, equity and every good path" (Proverbs 2:6, 7, 9).

"Trust in the LORD with all your heart, and lean not on your own understanding; in all your ways acknowledge Him, and He shall direct your paths" (Proverbs 3:5, 6).

"The heart of the righteous studies how to answer" (Proverbs 15:28a).

"The heart of the wise teaches his mouth, and adds learning to his lips" (Proverbs 16:23).

"Beware lest anyone cheat you through philosophy and empty deceit, according to the tradition of men, according to the basic principles of the world, and not according to Christ" (Colossians 2:8).

"If any of you lacks wisdom, let him ask of God, who gives to all liberally and without reproach, and it will be given to him" (James 1:5).

In context, this verse from James is talking about wisdom concerning trials.

When You Can't Sleep

Nighttime is the hardest, isn't it? Worry wants to settle in your heart for the night. Anxiety churns in your stomach. Heartache dampens your pillow with tears. Sometimes it seems you keep praying the same plea over and over again like a chant: *Please bring my loved one back home. Please help my loved one return to You before it's too late.* God's Word is better than warm milk. In fact, God promises that seeking His wisdom will chase away the nightly fears and give us sweet sleep (Proverbs 3:24). It will chase the doubts away. Raymond Edman said, "Never doubt in the darkness what God has shown you in the light." Keeping a Bible on the nightstand makes it easy to seek God's guidance during the dark night of the soul.

When You Can't Lift Up Your Head

Sometimes the choices of our dearest loved ones can bring shame upon the family. Whether it was an act of impropriety or cruelty, or whether they just gave up during a difficult time, we're the ones answering the questions. The conversation might go like this: "So where do your folks live now?" "Oh, my mom lives in Chicago and my dad lives in Miami." "What? They split up? What happened?" "My mom had an affair. They divorced. It was ugly." Or the conversation might go like this: "Your son's in college? That's great! Which church does he attend there?" "Well, none currently. He sorta has some issues he's trying to work through."

The pain resurfaces, and it's hard to talk about (again), to answer the questions, to try not to make excuses for them or defend them or protect them, to ask for prayers, to assure everyone you're not giving up hope. It can be wearying. When the worst thing that can happen happens, disgrace and embarrassment can make it hard to hold our head up as others learn about it.

Sheer exhaustion can also make it hard to hold our head up. No telling the number of hours spent in prayer and pleading and trying to be strong. Trying to hang on to joy can seem to get tougher. Every time we paste on a smile for a fun fellowship or determine not to cry during the singing in worship, our strength can seem to seep out a little bit more.

David wrote Psalm 3 when he was fleeing from Absalom. He was on the run, so there was fear involved. But he was also grieving. His very own son had turned against him and against God. What did David do? He relied on God to help him face each new day (v. 5). He cried to God for comfort (v. 4). But especially notice verse 3. "But You, O LORD, are a shield for me, my glory and the One who lifts up my head." Even though others were talking about David and speculating about him (v. 2), God was his shield, his protection. Even though he felt the shame of having his son behave in such an abominable fashion, God was his glory. And even though he was weighed down, God lifted up David's head. How beautiful! Let us remember what David knew: "Your blessing is upon Your people" (v. 8).

How to Seek God's Word

Prayerfully

The psalmist prayed, "Open my eyes, that I may see wondrous things from Your law" (Psalm 119:18). As we open the Bible, we can pray for wisdom, clarity, and guidance. How thrilling to think that we can talk to the very Author of the Book anytime we want!

Diligently

In relation to God's will, we see words that imply diligent effort on our part. We're to meditate on it day and night (Psalm 1:2). We're to seek

Him with our whole heart so we won't wander from His commandments (119:10). In Psalm 119 alone, notice some of the words used to describe what we're to do with the Word: meditate and contemplate (v. 15), cling (v. 31), walk and delight in (v. 35), long for (v. 40), trust (v. 42), keep (v. 69), learn (v. 73), and never forget (v. 93). Sporadic study is inadequate. Turning to the Bible only in times of trouble doesn't demonstrate trust or delight. We must seek God's guidance through diligent Bible study.

Respectfully

This is so important as we consider how God views sin and how He wants us to act when someone willfully engages in it. Respecting God's Word means that we recognize it as the final authority. It is Christ's words that will judge us (John 12:48–50), not any man's opinion. It's dangerous to try to "consider in a new light" what God has already settled on, even when it involves a loved one. For instance, some have changed their views concerning marriage, divorce, and remarriage after a loved one ended up in an unscriptural marriage. Some have adopted society's view toward homosexuality after a loved one embraced that lifestyle. And some have swallowed Satan's lie—"God just wants him/them/me to be happy"—to excuse sinful behavior. We can't twist the Scriptures to save our loved ones! We must be careful not to adapt our beliefs to our loved one's situation. God's Word is the final authority. Accepting that truth doesn't mean we're condemning a loved one. Each will be judged according to his deeds (Romans 2:6; Revelation 20:12, 13).

Respecting God's Word also means we will honor what it teaches about church discipline. The elders are charged with the heavy responsibility of keeping watch over the flock, and sometimes that involves practicing church discipline (Matthew 18:15-17; 1 Corinthians 5:11; 2 Thessalonians 3:6-15). It is very painful indeed when the one being "marked" is a loved one. What should our attitude be? We should fall on our knees and thank God for courageous elders who love souls enough to practice tough love! God loves our loved ones even more than we do. He knows what's best for them. He wants them back in His fold. Why would we want to interfere with God's plan when His chastening is for their own good (Hebrews 12:5–11)? If your loved one was disciplined, thank your elders. Thank them for their time and their prayers, and know beyond the shadow of a doubt that their actions were not taken lightly. Don't get angry or accuse them of being hateful. Respect them and respect God's Word.

"Your word is a lamp to my feet and a light to my path" (Psalm 119:105). Lamps and lights are needed in the dark. When the way is dark, it is essential that we seek guidance from God's Word.

ᨒFaith in Actionᨒ

Ask a friend or family member to do a shared Bible study with you. Choose together which Bible book you will study. Each of you will read a chapter a day and jot down your thoughts about what you read. At the end of the week, email your notes to each other (if that seems overwhelming, start with one chapter a week). This will hold you accountable to consistent Bible study and cause you to study deeper since you know you'll be sharing your insights with someone. Plus, you'll enjoy reading another person's thoughts about the same verses you studied.

Apply Your Heart (Proverbs 2:2)

1. Read 2 Thessalonians 2:16, 17. What two things has God already done for us? What two things can we ask Him to do for us? How will this help us reach out to those who have fallen away?

2. Proverbs 2:1–5 is an if/then statement. Bible study is not passive! List the eight words that show the action we're to take if we want to understand the fear of the Lord and find the knowledge of God. You might want to circle these words in your Bible, too.

3. There are 176 verses in Psalm 119, and almost all of them refer to God's Word. The writer used different words to describe the Word of God. Do some research to find their meanings.

    a.   commandments
    b.   judgments
    c.   law
    d.   precepts
    e.   statutes
    f.   testimonies

4. For your personal Bible study, create a simple chart with two columns. Title one column "The Student," and title the other column "The Word." Read through Psalm 119. When a verse mentions something the student should do, write it under that column. When a verse mentions something that the Word does for the student, write it under that column. For instance, in verse 1, the student's responsibility toward the Word is to "walk in" it. In verse 25, the Word "revives" us.

A Wife's Perspective

Her story: "My ex-husband left me and the church eleven years ago."

Scriptures she's relied on: Psalm 46:1–3; Isaiah 49:13; Psalm 9:9; 18:2; James 5:13; Jeremiah 29:11; Isaiah 40:31; Romans 8:28; 1 Corinthians 13:12; and especially Ecclesiastes 7:14 and James 1:2–4

Advice she'd offer to someone in a similar situation: "When I met my ex-husband, he was not a Christian. I refused to marry him until he became a Christian. Looking back, I wish I had handled things differently. I fear he was baptized just so I would marry him. We did Bible study together, and the youth minister worked with him. As long as things worked out well in our marriage, he was faithful. But when he would decide to be unfaithful to our wedding vows, he would be unfaithful at church. Eventually he didn't care anymore and quit going to church at all. He also began cheating more."

Additional thoughts: "My grandpa was not a Christian when my grandmother married him. At first she stayed on him about being a Christian, and it would just make him angry. Finally she stopped talking to him about it, and she caught him at the barn reading the Bible. He became a Christian when he was ready and convicted in his heart. He even served as an elder for years, right up until his death. He was a wonderful Christian man. I feel that nagging or giving ultimatums to loved ones to become a Christian does not make a true Christian. It is superficial, and what good is that if it's not one's own desire and choice?"

Chapter Five

Keep Praying

"BUT WHEN IN THEIR TROUBLE THEY TURNED TO THE LORD
GOD OF ISRAEL, AND SOUGHT HIM, HE WAS FOUND BY THEM."
2 CHRONICLES 15:4

When Jesus was praying in the Garden of Gethsemane, His disciples were supposed to be on watch. They couldn't do it. They were so tired. They weren't strong enough. They let Jesus down and then let Him down again in the exact same way. Jesus said that their spirit was willing, but their flesh was weak. What did Jesus tell them to do? "Watch and pray, lest you enter into temptation" (Matthew 26:41). When He told them to watch, He was telling them to get back to what they were supposed to be doing. When He told them to pray, He was telling them how to protect and fortify themselves while they were watching. Prayer is powerful.

Warning, comforting, upholding, pursuing, and being patient are the things we find ourselves doing when someone we love has fallen away. These are also the very things Paul told the elders at Thessalonica to do. "Warn those who are unruly, comfort the fainthearted, uphold the weak, be patient with all ... always pursue what is good both for yourselves and for all" (1 Thessalonians 5:14, 15). And it was in the context of this inspired guidance that Paul advised, "Pray without ceasing" (v. 17). In fact, it's notable that the first five (warning, comforting, upholding, pursuing, being patient with all) are things the leaders were to do for others.

Paul followed that up with some essential things they would need to do for themselves: rejoice, pray, give thanks, hold fast, and abstain (vv. 16–22). These would fortify the leaders for their important tasks. Rejoicing in all circumstances, praying constantly, and giving thanks in everything would keep their minds positive in potentially discouraging situations. Clinging to what is good and avoiding anything evil would protect their own souls when tempted to tolerate sin or modify God's teachings. We need fortification and protection as we reach out to those who have turned away from God.

Prayer is the ultimate litmus test because it is colored by our attitude. The command to pray in 1 Thessalonians 5:17 is sandwiched between the commands to rejoice and be thankful. We're to have a joyful, prayerful, thankful mentality, especially when working with others, "for this is the will of God in Christ Jesus for you" (v. 18). It's too easy to get caught up in the exact opposite. Perhaps we feel unable to rejoice because we are filled with anxiety or discouragement. After praying endlessly for someone without seeing any "results," it's tempting to think God no longer hears or cares. And instead of being thankful, we become resentful. What can we do? Rejoice, pray, and give thanks anyway.

Wise Words from the Pen of Paul

Ed Cole said, "Wishing will never be a substitute for prayer." Paul knew something about the importance of prayer in difficult situations. He had experienced quite a bit of trouble himself. Turn to 2 Corinthians 11:23–28 and notice the specific trials he faced. As we look at the list, we see that his difficulties would've included feelings of fear, disappointment in those he cared about, being treated unfairly, weariness, discouragement, and physical exhaustion. The very last thing he lists as one of his trials is his "deep concern for all the churches." He loved them and worried about the condition of their souls, and it took its toll on him. Sound familiar? Oh, we can certainly understand fear, disappointment, exhaustion, and worry. Can we rejoice, pray, and give thanks anyway? Paul could. He even wrote,

Not that I speak in regard to need, for I have learned in <u>whatever state</u> I am, to be content: I know how to be abased, and I know how to abound. <u>Everywhere</u> and in <u>all things</u> I have learned both to be full and to be hungry, both to abound and to suffer need. I can do <u>all things</u> through Christ who strengthens me. (Philippians 4:11–13)

No matter what Paul faced, he learned to be content because of the strength he found in Christ. How did Paul get that strength from Christ? I believe the answer is found in what he wrote earlier in the chapter.

Be anxious for <u>nothing</u>, but in <u>everything</u> by prayer and supplication, with thanksgiving, let your requests be made known to God; and the peace of God, which surpasses all understanding, will guard your hearts and minds through Christ Jesus. (Philippians 4:6, 7)

There are two commands in this passage.

Be anxious for nothing.

Here we are told exactly what we are to be worried about—nothing. In other words, do not be filled with cares. Don't worry about anything. Does this mean we're not supposed to worry about people we love? It's notable that the Philippians letter was about relationships. There was disharmony in the congregation. Paul had to remind them to put others first (2:3) and to quit complaining and disputing (v. 14). Paul told a couple of women in particular, Euodia and Syntyche, to "stand fast in the Lord" and "to be of the same mind" (4:1, 2). There was strife among these women who formerly served alongside Paul (v. 3). Their focus turned from promoting the gospel to selfish pursuits. What did Paul tell the church members who were dealing with all of this? Be anxious for nothing, and …

Let your requests be made known to God.

Instead of worrying, we pray. We tell God what we most desire. Of course, we've been praying since day one. That was probably the first thing we thought of doing. It was natural to turn to God in our distress. But remember the good quote, "If you only pray when you're in trouble ... you're in trouble." However, if the months turn into years, don't worry. Keep praying. There are three prepositional phrases that describe the command to let our requests be made known to God:

> » WHEN? "In everything"—the totality of life, for every reason, in every season.
> » WHAT? "By prayer and supplication"—prayer is the general term, while supplications are specific, ardent requests.
> » HOW? "With thanksgiving"—attitude again (remember 1 Thessalonians 5).

We have some personal questions we need to ask and answer honestly. Am I praying about everything still? Am I praying with a thankful heart, even when it seems God isn't listening?

When we pray, then we will have the peace of God. Scholars describe this word "peace" as "to have no worries" or "to be without trouble."[1] Do you see how that works? Don't worry. Pray, and then God will take away your worries. And the verse gets even more beautiful. This peace of God will guard our hearts and minds. To guard means to protect, to keep safe from danger. We know the dangers—discouragement, resentment, bitterness, doubt, and sin. When we keep praying, the peace of God keeps protecting. Our hearts and minds do need this protection. "Mind" includes our thoughts, reasoning, and understanding, while "heart" is the source of those thoughts. Just as he did in Philippians 4:13, Paul acknowledged again here that this is all made possible through Christ Jesus. All spiritual blessings are found in Christ (Ephesians 1:3). Whenever you're tempted to stop talking to God, remember that prayer brings protecting peace. As John Bunyan said, "Pray often, for prayer is a shield to the soul, a sacrifice to God, and a scourge to Satan."

---

1 J. Louw and E.A. Nida, *Greek-English Lexicon of the New Testament: Based on Semantic Domains*, electronic ed. of 2nd ed. (New York: United Bible Societies, 1996).

Keep praying for the sake of the wayward. Our prayers only have to outlast their unfaithfulness by one day. Continued prayer will build trust with the wayward, demonstrate our hope, and glorify God. Keep praying for your sake. It will remove anxiety, strengthen and protect you, and keep you close to God.

As we pray for others, let's not forget to pray with others. We can ask our sisters in Christ to pray for us and tell them we're praying for them. Better yet, we can pull them aside and pray with them. A strong church prays together often! And surely we want to let the wayward know that we are continuing to pray for them and will never stop. There's power in prayer!

⁓Faith in Action⁓

Open your Bible to Philippians 4. John Moore, who preaches for the Dripping Springs Church of Christ in Texas, shared these points. In the margin of your Bible, write "pray right" next to verse 6, "think right" next to verse 8, and "do right" next to verse 9.

Think of someone you know who also has a loved one who has turned away from God. Spend some time in prayer for the one who fell away, and then call the person you know and tell them you prayed for their loved one.

Apply Your Heart (Proverbs 2:2)

1. When praying "with thanksgiving," what are some specific blessings you can express gratitude for as you pray for those who have fallen away?

2. After praying for years for a loved one, a discouraged sister lost hope and said, "I don't think I can ever pray to God again." What would you say to encourage her? What scriptures would you share with her to help her see that God still cares?

3. The Godhead is involved!

  a. Read 1 Peter 5:6–11. According to verse 10, what four things will God Himself do for you?

  b. According to Hebrews 9:24, what will Christ do for you?

  c. According to Romans 8:26, what will the Holy Spirit do for you?

4. What did these righteous men do during times of difficulty and discouragement?

  a. Job—Job 16:20; 42:10

  b. Elijah—1 Kings 19:4, 5

  c. David—Psalm 28:6, 7

5. In a recent sermon, Neal Pollard said, "The Christians in Hebrews were urged to have boldness and confidence no matter what adversities they faced." What were the Christians told to do with that boldness and confidence?

  a. Hebrews 3:6

  b. Hebrews 4:16

  c. Hebrews 10:35

Without Ceasing

By Kathy Pollard

I said a prayer for you again,
I said a prayer for you.
My cares released, God gave me peace,
I said a prayer for you.

I breathed a prayer for you again,
I breathed a prayer for you.
I love your soul, I want you whole,
I breathed a prayer for you.

I cried a prayer for you again,
I cried a prayer for you.
He loves you more, He will restore
I cried a prayer for you.

I thought a prayer for you again,
I thought a prayer for you.
It reached God's ears for years, for years,
I thought a prayer for you.

I begged a prayer for you again,
I begged a prayer for you,
As long as I'm breathing, in prayer I'm believing,
I begged a prayer for you.

A Best Friend's Perspective

THEIR STORY: "My best friend has been unfaithful for about a year."

SCRIPTURES THEY HAVE RELIED ON: Mostly comforting scriptures like 2 Corinthians 1:1–3.

ADVICE THEY'D OFFER TO SOMEONE IN A SIMILAR SITUATION: "Never give up! You never know what your example can do and the light you possess. Although it's heartbreaking, we have a God who understands (Hebrews 4:15)."

HOW IT'S AFFECTED THEIR RELATIONSHIP: "Sadly, our relationship is in pieces. When you no longer possess that common fellowship with the person you held so dear, it seems it will never be the same. I have not lost hope, though. Sometimes it's hard to encourage myself to continue our relationship, but I try to remember how God is patient with me. I don't understand how someone could walk away from the truth. I hope and pray every day that I can encourage her and bring her back to the fold. Sadly, most days it feels impossible."

Chapter Six

Let Go of the Guilt

"THE SON SHALL NOT BEAR THE GUILT OF THE FATHER,
NOR THE FATHER BEAR THE GUILT OF THE SON."

EZEKIEL 18:20

Parents of unfaithful children, this chapter is for you. The Bible does say, "Train up a child in the way he should go, and when he is old he will not depart from it" (Proverbs 22:6). This verse has caused some to feel overly accountable for their wayward sons or daughters. Or perhaps some parents have been unfeelingly accused of spiritual neglect or lack of discipline. Mothers take to heart careless comments about their children. Fathers feel burdened when it comes to the spiritual well-being of their children. Mothers have given 100 percent, so 100 percent of their hearts ache as they ask questions: "Where did I go wrong? What could I have done better? What happened?"

Sarah Fallis, author and ladies speaker, said,

Having a loved one leave the Lord is so tragic, and such a difficult situation, but Christian parents (especially mothers) who have children who are unfaithful bear a much heavier burden because of the love we had for them even before they were born. Sometimes, it can be devastating.[1]

Guilt is an unwelcome companion. It weighs heavily on our hearts,

1 S. Fallis, "More Thoughts," email to the author, August 8, 2013.

steals our peace, and wreaks havoc on our health. In describing the side effects of guilt, Michael McKee, PhD, wrote:

> If you're guilty you're probably getting stressed. If your body releases stress chemicals, it puts you at risk for minor stuff like headaches and backaches. It also contributes to cardiovascular disease and gastrointestinal disorders. It can even have a negative impact on the immune system over time. It contributes significantly to depression, as it very often involves a negative view of self, and to anxiety.[1]

Some Christian parents will struggle with guilt over their sins. Perhaps they really did neglect the upbringing of their children through misplaced priorities or sinful behaviors. But most Christian parents struggle with guilt, not over sin but a sense of failure. Mothers will look in the mirror and see a failure. They'll think, "I had one main job ... to raise my children to be faithful Christians ... and I failed. I failed!"

How to Deal with the Guilt

What can one do when feeling overwhelmed with guilt because of wayward children?

Take a closer look at Proverbs 22:6.

While preparing for this chapter, I thought an in-depth look at this verse would prove it does not mean exactly what it says. I was wrong. If the verse were to be written literally, according to the meaning of the Hebrew words, it would read, "Dedicate a young man on the path; surely, surely, as an old man, he cannot turn aside/fall away from it." So, in fact, the verse does mean exactly what it says. But we still must take a closer look.

The book of Proverbs is in a section of the Bible recognized as poetry. The point of the proverbs is to help readers grow in wisdom, knowledge,

---

1 Louise Chang, "Is Guilt Getting the Best of You?", WebMD, May 8 2006, accessed May 18, 2017, http://www.webmd.com/balance/features/is-guilt-getting-best-of-you.

and instruction (Proverbs 1:1-6). There are many guidelines for parents (22:6; 29:15), wives (21:9; 31:10-31), children (1:8), and even friends (17:17; 27:17). To say that Proverbs 22:6 is an absolute guarantee is to contradict the Bible truth that one can fall from grace (which will be discussed more in chapter eight of this book). We must conclude then that, in Proverbs 22:6, Solomon was using hyperbole, a common device in poetry, to prove a point. What was his point? Children will have a much greater chance of choosing to remain faithful if we bring them up in the Lord (see also Ephesians 6:1-4). Jeff Martin, a brother in Christ, said something very helpful in light of Proverbs 22:6:

> Sometimes it's hard for people to reconcile what they read in Proverbs versus the "inconsistencies" they observe in the world. The truths Solomon expressed are a great current pulling men in a certain direction—it can be resisted, avoided, delayed, but it always pulls one way. There is always more than one variable at play, and when time and chance happen to every man (Ecclesiastes 9:11), sometimes the foolish are exalted and the lazy made rich. It doesn't mean the proverb is not true in that case; a sloth accumulating wealth must struggle against many things. His lack of motivation, lack of time, lack of effort are all constantly dragging him toward ruin and he's swimming against the stream. In the same way, a child who is raised in the Lord but departs from the faith must overcome many things: the advice of his parents, the truths he was taught in the scriptures, the good examples set by his family and friends, the influence held on him by the same, etc. We must do what is right, and be spiritually minded enough to not let what happens in this temporary life affect our pursuit of the eternal one.

Try not to bear the guilt of another.

"The soul who sins shall die. The son shall not bear the guilt of the father, nor the father bear the guilt of the son. The righteousness of the righteous shall be upon himself, and the wickedness of the wicked shall be upon himself" (Ezekiel 18:20). This entire chapter in Ezekiel is about some confusion the Israelites had about sons bearing the guilt of their fathers and vice versa. God wanted them to understand that each one will be held accountable for his own actions, and his alone. Notice also, "When a righteous man turns away from his righteousness and commits iniquity ... shall he live? All the righteousness which he has done shall not be remembered; because of the unfaithfulness of which he is guilty and the sin which he has committed, because of them he shall die" (v. 24). The Lord concludes with "Therefore I will judge you, O house of Israel, every one according to his ways" (v. 30). Just as children cannot stand in judgment on the basis of their parents' goodness, parents will not stand in judgment on the basis of their grown children's waywardness.

Remember biblical examples of those who fell away.

Solomon was the son of David, who was the "man after [God's] own heart" (1 Samuel 13:14; Acts 13:22). Solomon was given a miraculous amount of wisdom (1 Kings 3:5–14) and even penned three books in the Old Testament. And yet, in his old age, he turned away from God and embraced idolatry.

> For it was so, when Solomon was old, that his wives turned his heart after other gods; and his heart was not loyal to the LORD his God, _as was the heart of his father David._ ... Solomon did evil in the sight of the LORD, and did not fully follow the LORD, _as did his father David._ (1 Kings 11:4, 6)

Here's an example of a son who went wayward despite his father's tender heart and genuine faithfulness. Sadly, David had multiple children who were spiritual disappointments. Solomon started out strong. He even served God for most of his life. But then he allowed his weaknesses to rule his heart.

Joel and Abijah had a godly father. They were the sons of Samuel, who served as a prophet, judge, and priest. But Joel and Abijah were listed as the reason the Israelites wanted a king.

> Now it came to pass when Samuel was old that he made his sons judges over Israel. ... But his sons _did not walk in his ways;_ they turned aside after dishonest

gain, took bribes, and perverted justice. Then all the elders of Israel gathered together and came to Samuel at Ramah, and said to him, "Look, you are old, and your sons do not walk in your ways. Now make us a king to judge us like all the nations." (1 Samuel 8:1-5)

Samuel was a tremendously good man. In addition to the accounts we have in the Old Testament of his service, he was also mentioned by Peter in Acts 3:24, by Paul in Acts 13:20, and included in the "Faith Hall of Fame" in Hebrews 11:32. And yet his boys did not "walk in his ways." Despite their father's faithfulness, Joel and Abijah chose to abandon the path of righteousness.

What about Judas Iscariot, the son of Simon? This man was one of the elite Twelve, an apostle of Jesus Christ. He followed Jesus, learned from Him, spent time in His presence, and saw His miracles firsthand. And yet, he allowed Satan to enter his heart on at least two different occasions (Luke 22:3; John 13:27), and this was before and during the Passover meal. What better influence could Judas possibly have had than the very Son of God? What better environment could he have been in than the meaningful Passover meal, surrounded by godly men? Judas is an example of a man who, even in the best circumstances, allowed his fleshly desires (greed) to get the best of him (Matthew 26:47-49; 27:1-5). Did Jesus feel responsible? Should Jesus have forced Judas to do the right thing? No. God wants voluntary obedience from all of His children.

There are many other examples mentioned in the Bible of those who turned away from God. Some did have parents who were ungodly, but many had parents who tried to live a life pleasing to God.

Consider some practical thoughts.

First, children brought up in the same home can turn out completely different spiritually. One mother has four children. Two of them are faithful, and two aren't, even though they were all brought up in the same home with the same teachings, rules, and parental guidance. They were each shown the same amount of love, taken to worship each week, patiently disciplined, and diligently taught the Word. What happened? Simply put, two of them chose to embrace what the world has to offer instead.

Second, Satan is actively seeking to destroy God's people. He reaches them through their weaknesses. Ananias and Sapphira, because of their pride of life, sought glory for themselves (Acts 5:3). Before that weak, fateful moment, were they hardworking members of the Lord's church? Remember, Satan tempts married couples, according to 1 Corinthians 7:5. How many faithful men (preachers even) have given in to the lust of the flesh by committing adultery when the temptress came along? Satan tries to hinder the work of the saints, according to 1 Thessalonians 2:18. The saints! The ones who are saved, who belong to God! Satan targets them. He uses devices to take advantage of them (2 Corinthians 2:11). He's called the tempter (Matthew 4:3), and he deceives the whole world (Revelation 12:9). Satan is every Christian's enemy their entire life.

And third, circumstances may momentarily weaken the resolve of even the most faithful of Christians. Sometimes tragedies occur that cause us to question whether or not the Christian life is "worth it." The unexpected death of a child or being abandoned or betrayed by a spouse can cause such overwhelming grief and anguish that a Christian may flounder around. They may lash out at God. And some just never muster up the strength to find their way back home. Kristy Woodall, a preacher's wife and ladies speaker, commented:

> This is pure speculation, but I wonder if we should consider that Moses, the great servant of God, disobeyed Him (by striking the rock) right after the death of his sister. Perhaps something to keep in mind when tragedy comes your way. Keep the faith!

These practical thoughts are meant to encourage any who struggle with guilt over a loved one who has fallen away. The point is that we can't make others live right and do right. Each of us will face and fight our own battles. We must choose to remain faithful even under the most dire circumstances. We can pray for those we love. We can teach and admonish.

We can set a good example. But ultimately, they, and only they, will give an account for their waywardness.

Get into God's Word.

As always, the Bible has everything we need for life and godliness (2 Peter 1:3). Spend some time soaking in God's promises. Let His Word soothe your fears of failure. Here are some Scriptures to start you off:

Psalm 37:23—"The steps of a good man are ordered by the Lord, and He delights in his way." God knows our hearts. He knows we want the best for those we love. If we are doing our best, He will take care of the rest.

Psalm 60:11-12—"Give us help from trouble, for the help of man is useless. Through God we will do valiantly, for it is He who shall tread down our enemies." It is only by God's strength and might that good reigns. Satan is persistent, but God has the power to overcome.

Lamentations 3:22-24—"Through the Lord's mercies we are not consumed, because His compassions fail not. They are new every morning; great is Your faithfulness. 'The Lord is my portion,' says my soul, 'therefore I hope in Him!'" God's love and mercy are greater than our guilt and fear. Each morning He grants is another day to rest in His hope.

Micah 7:7, 8—"Therefore I will look to the Lord; I will wait for the God of my salvation; my God will hear me. Do not rejoice over me, my enemy; when I fall, I will arise; when I sit in darkness, the Lord will be a light to me." Keep looking up. Let God bear your burden of guilt. He listens. He raises us up. His light dispels the darkness.

Romans 8:31—"What then shall we say to these things? If God is for us, who can be against us?" This is one verse in an entire chapter of hope for the Christian! God knows we struggle, but He promises to be with us. His love is great and unending, and He desires the best for our loved ones even more than we do. No past and no guilt can take that assurance away from us.

2 Corinthians 2:14, 15—"Now thanks be to God who always leads us in triumph in Christ, and through us diffuses the fragrance of His knowl-

edge in every place. For we are to God the fragrance of Christ among those who are being saved and among those who are perishing." Instead of drowning in guilt, we can "[diffuse] the fragrance of His knowledge in every place." That is our job. Satan wants us to forget that.

It seems appropriate to end this chapter with additional words by Sarah Fallis, concerning a wayward loved one.

> *Here are some things I know: Prayer helps. God cares. He knows our hurts. He can work, but He can't work against [our] free will. And, the biggest thing that gives me hope is: THE LAST CHAPTER ... HAS NOT BEEN WRITTEN!!! (We have all known faithful people who have left the Lord, and we've all known unfaithful ones who have come back to Him.) I will fight in prayer and I won't give up.*[1]

∾Faith in Action∾

If you're struggling with guilt or a sense of failure because of a wayward child (or even spouse or sibling), write out your feelings in a letter. Explain again that the only thing that matters to you is where that loved one will spend eternity. Seal the letter with a prayer, decide whether it would be wise to mail it off, and try to let it go.

---

1 S. Fallis, "More Thoughts," email to the author, August 8, 2013.

Apply Your Heart (Proverbs 2:2)

1. Discuss ways to handle thoughtless comments made to parents of wayward children. How should you reply when people say things that hurt, lay blame, etc.?

2. No one hurts the same or has the same situation. How can we be more supportive of those who have had loved ones fall away? What are some ways we can encourage them?

3. Look for other examples in the Bible of godly parents who had children turn away from God. What can we learn from them?

A Father's Perspective

HIS STORY: "My daughter has been unfaithful for nine months. If feels like longer."

SCRIPTURES HE'S RELIED ON: Passages regarding the specific sin she's involved in and Matthew 6:33

ADVICE HE'D OFFER TO SOMEONE IN A SIMILAR SITUATION: "Do what God wants. Don't compromise truth. Trust Him. Be patient."

ADDITIONAL THOUGHTS: "It's easy to get caught up in the 'drama' of the situation, to let frustration become anger, and compromise to creep in. DON'T LET IT! And pray, pray, pray."

Chapter Seven

Warn the Wanderer

"Brethren, if anyone among you wanders from
the truth, and someone turns him back,
let him know that he who turns a sinner
from the error of his way will
save a soul from death and
cover a multitude of sins."
James 5:19, 20

Kevin Rhodes, when preaching a lesson called "God's Problems with the People," said, "Sin has gone from being shamed, to being ignored, to being accepted, to being celebrated! The moment we begin taking sin lightly is the moment we take what Jesus did lightly." The world doesn't view sin the way God does. It seems the only "sin" is intolerance of the sinful practices of others! But we as Christians must continue to abhor sin. "You who love the Lord, hate evil!" (Psalm 97:10). "Abhor what is evil. Cling to what is good" (Romans 12:9). We must see sin as the great separator. "But your iniquities have separated you from your God; and your sins have hidden His face from you, so that He will not hear" (Isaiah 59:2). And we must remember that willful sin carries heavy consequences. "For the wages of sin is death" (Romans 6:23). Those who engage in sin will not inherit the kingdom of God (Galatians 5:19–21). With this accurate view of sin in mind, we will want to warn those who have turned away from God. Fearful for their souls, we will not hesitate to try to convince them of the danger they are facing. When we view sin the way God does, we understand our role as watchmen.

Guidelines for Warning the Wayward

God sent Ezekiel to His wayward children. They were already in Babylonian captivity, a divine punishment for their idolatry. But they were still rebellious at heart and needed to be warned. God told Ezekiel, "I have made you a watchman for the house of Israel; therefore hear a word from My mouth, and give them warning from Me" (Ezekiel 3:17). The children of Israel were enslaved because of their sin; our wayward loved ones are enslaved to their sin (John 8:34; Romans 6:16). From Ezekiel 3, we learn several important and helpful guidelines for warning the wayward.

Where do we start?

"Son of man, receive into your heart all My words that I speak to you, and hear with your ears" (Ezekiel 3:10). God wanted Ezekiel to hear all of His words so he would know what to say to the captives. We must begin with the Word of God. We may have opinions and inclinations with regard to the sinful activities of the ones who have fallen away. We may wish for God's leniency, and thus, our hopeful message neglects to convey the seriousness of their situation. Our opinions, thoughts, and feelings do not matter and, in fact, can be misleading. It doesn't matter what we think or say or even what our preacher says. We must use God's Word only as our authority and guide. What does the Bible say about repentance? What does the Bible say about marriage, divorce, and remarriage or any other situation that can cause one to reject God? Let us always first go to God's Word before even attempting to warn the wayward. We don't want to lead them even further astray!

What is our responsibility?

"Go to them. Speak My words to them. Give them a warning from Me." That's what God told Ezekiel to do for the wayward children of Israel (3:4, 17). That's what we must do as well. It is our responsibility to warn.

If we don't, who will? "When I say to the wicked, 'You shall surely die,' and you give him no warning, nor speak to warn the wicked from his wicked way, to save his life, that same wicked man shall die in his iniquity; but his blood I will require at your hand" (v. 18). Referring to them as "wicked" makes it sound like it doesn't really apply to our loved ones. Maybe it's just about the evil people in the world who never followed God in the first place. But no, these words were said about the children of Israel, God's people. When they turned away from Him, they became wicked. As harsh as it sounds, anyone who falls away from God has become "the wicked," who are in danger and in need of warning.

It is not our responsibility to make the wayward listen or repent. God told Ezekiel, "He who hears, let him hear; and he who refuses, let him refuse; for they are a rebellious house" (3:27). God wants us to warn them, but their response isn't our responsibility. "Yet, if you warn the wicked, and he does not turn from his wickedness, nor from his wicked way, he shall die in his iniquity; but you have delivered your soul" (v. 19).

What if we don't think they're ready or willing to listen?

Here's what God told Ezekiel about that. "And go, get to the captives, to the children of your people, and speak to them and tell them, 'Thus says the Lord GOD,' whether they hear, or whether they refuse" (3:11). Whether or not we think the wayward will listen, it is still our responsibility to go, to get to them, and to speak to them about what God says. God even told Ezekiel, "But the house of Israel will not listen to you, because they will not listen to Me; for all the house of Israel are impudent and hard-hearted" (v. 7). The New American Standard Bible reads "stubborn and obstinate." Their hearts weren't open or tender, yet God still sent Ezekiel to plead with them.

Our Objectives as Watchmen

What do we hope to accomplish with the warnings? As with Ezekiel, there are multiple goals.

Remind Them of the Truth

The children of Israel (Judah specifically) had already seen the northern tribes go off into captivity and then disappear altogether. Had they forgotten? Why didn't they learn from Israel's example and consequences? Whatever the reason, God knew they needed another warning. God is longsuffering and wants all men to repent (2 Peter 3:9). Perhaps Satan, the father of lies, deceived them. Ezekiel reminded them of the truth: they were facing imminent judgment. They were in danger. Our wayward loved ones may have been deluded by the motto of this age—please self. They may have swallowed Satan's lies. We must remind them of the eternal truth: if they don't repent, they will face the consequences. The watchman warns the wicked to "save his life" so he won't "die in his iniquity" (Ezekiel 3:18, 19).

Remind Them Who God Is

"They shall know I am the LORD." This phrase appears over sixty times in the book of Ezekiel (see 6:7; 7:4, 9, 27; 13:9, 14, etc.). Having turned to idolatry, God's people forgot who He was. Over and over, God said to Ezekiel, "Tell them, 'Thus says the Lord GOD'" (3:11, 27). He wanted Ezekiel and the people to know that if they didn't heed His warning, they weren't rejecting Ezekiel; they were rejecting the Lord God. Just as a proper understanding of sin motivates us to warn the wayward, a proper understanding of God motivates the wayward to return to Him.

Remind Them of Their Accountability

Even though the entire nation of Israel was guilty, God pointed out their individual accountability. Any who turned away from righteousness would face the consequences of their sin. Conversely, any who turned away from their wickedness would "surely live" (Ezekiel 3:20, 21). Sometimes when loved ones fall away, they refuse to acknowledge their accountability. They blame their parents, their upbringing, an unfaithful spouse, a personal tragedy, or even the church. As was mentioned in the last chapter, God would later say to Ezekiel, "The soul who sins shall die.

The son shall not bear the guilt of the father, nor the father bear the guilt of the son. The righteousness of the righteous shall be upon himself, and the wickedness of the wicked shall be upon himself" (18:20). Part of our purpose in warning the wanderer is to remind them that each one of us will give an account in the day of judgment (Romans 14:12; 2 Corinthians 5:10; Hebrews 4:13).

Remind Them to Beware of False Teachers

The Israelites thought their punishment would be brief. Their hearts remained hard because they couldn't believe God would allow them to remain in captivity. After all, they were His people and He loved them. Jeremiah, also writing to the Israelites in Babylonian captivity, pointed out their delusion. He told them to build houses, plant gardens, marry, and have children because they had seventy years of captivity ahead of them (Jeremiah 29:5, 6, 10). But why did the Israelites believe in the first place that God would be easy on them? Because they were deceived by false prophets who simply told them what they wanted to hear (vv. 8, 9). How frightening to think that there are those who will tell our wayward loved ones what they want to hear! They will offer false peace. The wayward may relax, convinced that God just wants them to be happy, that His grace covers everything without any need to repent. We must warn the wanderer that there are those whose teaching leads to destruction, whether intentionally or not (2 Peter 2:1, 2).

Where We Find Our Strength

Ezekiel set about his task. He went to the captives and "sat where they sat, and remained there astonished among them seven days" before he ever said a word (Ezekiel 3:15). Why was he astonished? Some versions read "appalled" or "devastated." Was he working up courage or simply trying to let them know he cared by his presence? Perhaps he was dismayed by the message he had to give the people. Ezekiel "went in bitterness, in the heat of [his] spirit" (v. 14). This tells us more about his mindset. He was indignant, angry—even bitter. According to *The New American Commentary*,

"He may have been overwhelmed by the weight and unpleasantness of his assignment, especially the knowledge that the people would be generally unresponsive."[1] But Ezekiel went anyway. He relied on God's strength. God said: "Behold, I have made your face strong against their faces, and your forehead strong against their foreheads. Like adamant stone, harder than flint, I have made your forehead; do not be afraid of them, nor be dismayed by their looks, though they are a rebellious house" (vv. 8, 9). The people looked rebellious, and Ezekiel had to face them. Again, *The New American Commentary* suggests:

> *Opposition was pictured as coming from people with hardened faces. This implied a hardened will set against the word and will of God. God responded by promising the prophet that he would harden the forehead of Ezekiel so that it was like "hardest stone." The word "hardest stone" (v. 9) probably was reference to a diamond, the hardest stone known, and has been rendered "diamond" in some translations.*[2]

Does your loved one wear a rebellious countenance that reflects a hardened heart? Is it hard to face such anger and resentment? God will fortify us for the difficult task! It's painful to see loved ones stony-faced, but God will strengthen us as we try to soften their hearts with His message. By the way, the name Ezekiel means "God strengthens."

While love prompts us to warn those we care about, it's no easy task. And we need to realize that it may not turn out well. God told Ezekiel, "Surely they will put ropes on you and bind you with them, so that you cannot go out among them" (3:25). In their rebellious state, the people rejected Ezekiel's warning, even going so far as to physically prevent him from speaking to them. It may be that our wayward loved ones, while in their rebellious state, physically remove themselves from our presence. They may offer ultimatums: "As long as you're preaching at me, I want

---

1 L.E. Cooper, *Ezekiel*, electronic ed., Logos Library System: The New American Commentary (Nashville: Broadman & Holman Publishers, 2001), 83.

2 Ibid., 81.

nothing to do with you. Stay away from me." But God wants us to warn them anyway. What should we say? We can say what God told Ezekiel to say: "'As I live,' says the Lord GOD, 'I have no pleasure in the death of the wicked, but that the wicked turn from his way and live. Turn, turn from your evil ways! For why should you die, O house of Israel?'" (33:11).

∾Faith in Action∾

Explain to your wayward loved one that you've been studying Ezekiel and have been reminded of God's desire for us to warn those who have turned away from Him. If you've already warned your loved one, perhaps enough time has gone by to broach the subject again. Even if your loved one rejects your warning, tell them you continue to pray that they will "turn and live!"

Apply Your Heart (Proverbs 2:2)

1. Understanding how God sees sin motivates us to reach out to others. According to the following verses, how does God view sin?

    a.   Galatians 6:7–9

    b.   Hebrews 3:12–14

    c.   James 1:12–16

    d.   James 2:10

    e.   1 John 1:9

2. Discuss the three commands found in Galatians 6:1, 2. What are some practical ways we can apply them when reaching out to the wayward?

3. According to James 5:19, 20, what happens when someone brings back a sinner from his wandering?

4. Ezekiel 33 is another chapter devoted to the watchman. What can we learn about warning the wayward from the following verses?

    » vv. 2–5 _____

    » v. 6 _____

    » vv. 12, 13 _____

    » vv. 14–16 _____

    » vv. 17–20 _____

    » vv. 30–33 _____

A Brother's Perspective

His story: "My sister has been wayward for two years."

Scriptures he's relied on: Luke 15:17; 1 Corinthians 13:13; 2 Timothy 3:16; Psalm 23:3; 2 Peter 3:9; James 5:16

Advice he'd offer to someone in a similar situation: "God hears the prayers of a righteous person, so never stop praying on behalf of the lost person. Love covers a multitude of sins—both theirs and mine—so don't give off an air of highness. She knows what's right and wrong and doesn't need me to feel as though I'm judging her. I'm to love her by being God's tool in repentance."

Additional thoughts: "I truly believe that had she married someone who was a Christian, who loved God and desired to reach heaven together, this would not have happened. Not that we all don't have struggles of all kinds. But there is a huge disconnect in her husband's 'belief system' and God's. Therefore, she was pulled down by years of discouragement and lack of a common goal. Having nothing in common spiritually will eventually take its toll on your marriage."

Chapter Eight

Understand God's Grace

"LET US THEREFORE COME BOLDLY
TO THE THRONE OF GRACE,
THAT WE MAY OBTAIN MERCY AND
FIND GRACE TO HELP IN TIME OF NEED."
HEBREWS 4:16

Grace is a key word in Romans, appearing twenty-four times. Paul began the letter by saying, "Through [Jesus] we have received grace" (1:5). He also said, "Grace to you and peace from God our Father and the Lord Jesus Christ" (v. 7). This phrase is found in every single epistle Paul wrote. Grace was important to him, and he wanted his readers to have it. Grace has been defined as "unmerited favor" or "God's favor to the undeserving." There's even an acronym for it by an unknown author: **G**od's **R**iches **A**t **C**hrist's **E**xpense. Grace is a common word, but what does it mean for Christians? In light of our topic, what does it mean for the wayward? To help answer these questions, let's take a close look at a passage in which Paul had a great deal to say about grace. Open your Bible to Romans 5:12–21 and read it through; then continue with your reading of this book.

The Contrast

The first thing that stands out is the great contrast between sin and grace. In nearly every verse, there is a significant contrast pointed out.

It is summarized nicely in Romans 5:18:

> *Therefore, as through one man's offense judgment came to all men, resulting in condemnation, even so through one Man's righteous act the free gift came to all men, resulting in justification of life.*

To help see the contrast more vividly, consider the chart on the following page.

The contrast is as vivid as black and white. There's no blurring of the lines. There's no gray area. Sin is offensive and results in condemnation and death. We don't get to name something sin. God already did that. We don't determine that some sins are acceptable or tolerable. If the Bible says it's sin, it brings condemnation and death. Grace is abundant and results in justification and life. Just as we don't get to name sin, we don't get to define grace. God has already done that for us. He has already made clear how one receives the free gift of grace.

The Location of Grace

From our text, we see that grace is found in Jesus Christ. He is the access to this gift (Romans 5:1, 2). The abundance of grace is through Jesus Christ (v. 17). Grace brings eternal life through Jesus Christ (v. 21). It's even implied in verse 16, which tells us that grace brings justification, pointing back to the fact that we're justified by His blood (v. 9).

Other passages tell us that the location of grace is in Christ. "Grace that is in Jesus Christ" (2 Timothy 2:1). "We have redemption through His blood, the forgiveness of sins, according to the riches of His grace" (Ephesians 1:7). So those who are in Christ have the free gift of grace.

How do we know if we are in Christ? "For as many of you as were baptized into Christ have put on Christ" (Galatians 3:27). Baptism is the representation of the death, burial, and resurrection of Jesus Christ (Romans 6:1–4). This was the "obedient act" referred to in our text that brought about our grace (5:6–11, 18, 19)!

THE CONTRAST BETWEEN SIN AND GRACE Romans 5:12–21	
SIN	GRACE
"death through sin" (v. 12)	
"death spread to all men" (v. 12)	
"death reigned" (v. 14)	
	"free gift" (v. 15)
	"gift" (v. 15)
"many died" (v. 15)	"abounded to many" (v. 15)
	"gift" (v. 16)
	"free gift" (v. 16)
"judgment" (v. 16)	
"condemnation" (v. 16)	"justification" (v. 16)
	"abundance of grace" (v. 17)
	"gift of righteousness" (v. 17)
"death reigned" (v. 17)	"reign in life" (v. 17)
"judgment came to all men" (v. 18)	"free gift came to all men" (v. 18)
"condemnation" (v. 18)	"justification of life" (v. 18)
"many were made sinners" (v. 19)	"many will be made righteous" (v. 19)
"sin abounded" (v. 20)	"grace abounded much more" (v. 20)
"sin reigned in death" (v. 21)	"grace might reign ... to eternal life" (v. 21)

Misconceptions about the Gift of Grace

Grace is a common word, even in the secular world. It's in the title of some country songs, like "But for the Grace of God" by Keith Urban. In "My Life's Been a Country Song" by Chris Cagle, he sings about "true love and amazing grace ... raisin' Cain Friday nights, Sunday church to set it right!" Even Katy Perry has a song titled "By the Grace of God."

Just because most people are familiar with the word doesn't mean they understand it. There are some common misconceptions about grace.

Misconception #1: Grace is a free pass for sins of which I don't want to repent.

Some use grace as a "get out of jail free" card. They keep it in their back pocket until they need it. I have a personal family member who committed adultery and is now in an unscriptural marriage. At first he acknowledged that his actions were sinful. Now he claims that "God's grace covers it" because "God wants him to be happy." Paul specifically addressed this misconception about grace in the very next chapter. "What shall we say then? Shall we continue in sin that grace may abound? Certainly not! How shall we who died to sin live any longer in it?" (Romans 6:1, 2). The King James Version reads, "God forbid." Paul went on to discuss the fact that when we were set free from sin, we became slaves of righteousness (vv. 15–18).

Grace is not an excuse to continue in willful sin. Instead, according to our text, grace is directly tied to righteousness. It is the gift of righteousness (Romans 5:17). It came through a righteous act (v. 18). It came through an act of obedience so that all would be made righteous (v. 19). It reigns through righteousness (v. 21). Righteousness involves what is right, what God requires. Sin is the opposite of that. It is a transgression of what is right, what God requires. To continue in sin thinking that grace will cover it is to completely misunderstand and abuse God's grace. Paul explained that being under grace means living righteously before God. "And do not present your members as instruments of unrighteousness to sin, but present yourselves to God as being alive from the dead, and your members as instruments of righteousness to God. For sin shall not have dominion over you, for you are not under the law but under grace" (6:13, 14). John MacArthur said, "Grace does not grant permission to live in the flesh; it supplies power to live in the Spirit."

Some find it necessary to "redefine" God in order to make peace with their sinful lifestyles. They begin to view God as ONLY merciful and compassionate. But we must also consider God's holiness and His hatred of sin (Isaiah 6:3; Habakkuk 1:13). We can't embrace one and reject the other. Peter addressed this very thing in his first letter. It was as if he was writing specifically to my family member who claims that God's grace is covering his unscriptural marriage. "Therefore gird up the loins of your mind, be sober, and rest your hope fully upon the grace that is to be brought to you at the revelation of Jesus Christ; as obedient children, not conforming yourselves to the former lusts, as in your ignorance; but as He who called you is holy, you also be holy in all your conduct, because it is written, 'Be holy, for I am holy'" (1 Peter 1:13–16).

Misconception #2: I can't fall from grace.

The idea that one can't fall from grace is a man-made doctrine. It is not found in Scripture. The Bible teaches that we can, in fact, fall from grace. Consider the following verses:

HEBREWS 12:14–17—The Hebrews letter was addressed to Christians. The writer admonished them to pursue peace and holiness. If they didn't, notice what was to happen: "No one will see the Lord" (v. 14). They will "fall short of the grace of God" and "become defiled" (v. 15). The Hebrews writer then used the example of Esau as one who gave up his birthright for a morsel of food. Then, "when he wanted to inherit the blessing, he was rejected, for he found no place for repentance, though he sought it diligently with tears" (vv. 16, 17). Esau was already blessed, but because of foolish decisions, he lost the blessing. This passage warns Christians to be careful not to lose their eternal blessing either by neglecting to do certain good things or by neglecting to repent of sinful things.

2 PETER 2:15, 20–22—In this chapter, Peter warned of false teachers who would turn some away from the truth. When one comes to know Christ, it is possible for him to become entangled in the world again or to be overcome. Peter warned that "it would have been better for them not to have known the way of righteousness, than having known it, to turn from the holy commandment delivered to them." It seems that the idea of "once saved always saved" must then be a product of the false teachings that Peter warned against.

GALATIANS 5:1, 4—Paul explained that we enjoy freedom because of Christ but only as long as we "stand fast." Otherwise we can become "entangled again with a yoke of bondage." This is slavery to sin. Grace is freedom from sin, so to become slaves again to sin means it's possible to fall from grace. Paul went on to say, "You have become estranged from Christ ... you have *fallen from grace.*"

Misconception #3: There's not enough grace to cover my past.

While some abuse the gift of God's grace by using it as an excuse to sin, others have a hard time accepting God's grace for themselves. They don't feel worthy. Perhaps they're consumed with remorse over past sins. Maybe they made a poor choice in the past that can never be fixed or changed and they can't let go of the guilt long enough to accept God's forgiveness. In other words, they think God's grace is for everyone but them. They may say things like, "But you don't know what I've done."

That's the beauty of the words used to describe grace in Romans 5. Grace "abounded to many" (v. 15). There's an "abundance of grace" (v. 17). It came to "all men" (v. 18). And while "sin abounded, grace abounded much more" (v. 20). Grace is for everyone, and it's greater than our sin, as the old song claims.

The great apostle Paul had a past. Turn to 1 Timothy 1:12-15. He admitted that he was a blasphemer, a persecutor, and an insolent man. Some versions read "violent aggressor" instead of "insolent." This word is found only one other time in the New Testament. In Romans 1:30, it's listed right after "haters of God" and is "deserving of death" (v. 32). No wonder Paul referred to himself as the chief of sinners! Some versions read "foremost of all." But Paul said he obtained mercy because of three things found in Christ Jesus—faith, love, and grace. And when he mentioned grace, he used some hope-giving adjectives. It's not just grace; it's *abundant* grace. It's not just abundant grace; it's *exceedingly abundant* grace. God's grace is certainly bigger than our mistakes, our horrible choices, and our dark pasts. All we have to do is accept it by being in Christ and being Christlike.

The Power of Grace

All who have accepted God's grace should have been changed by it. Grace is powerful because of its influence in our lives and on our outlook. Twice in Romans 5 we're told that grace "reigns" (vv. 17, 21). The word "reign" means "to be king; rule over; control completely." Does grace rule your life? Does it control you completely? If so, you will notice its influence over your life, and so will others.

We have been saved by grace, and if that grace rules our lives, then ...

Our choices will reflect it.

Remember, grace and righteousness go hand in hand. No, we won't live perfectly. We will still slip up and sin occasionally. But the grace-governed Christian will strive diligently to walk in righteousness.

Our attitude will reflect it.

We will be joyful. How can one who has received such a gift not be happy and excited about it? We will be grateful. We'll thank God for His love and mercy. And we will be compassionate. We'll want to abound in grace. We'll be as compassionate toward others as God has been toward us, and that will cause us to be patient and forgiving. Philip Yancey said,

One who has been touched by grace will no longer look on those who stray as "those evil people" or "those poor people who need our help." Nor must we search for signs of "loveworthiness." Grace teaches us that God loves because of who God is, not because of who we are.

We'll want everyone to know about it.

Grace is too good to keep to ourselves. We'll want to share it with every non-Christian. We'll make every effort to reach out to the wayward, to impress upon them the power and tenderness of God's amazing grace.

What then is this gift of grace? According to Romans 5, it is the gift of salvation, justification, and eternal life. It is sufficient and abundant.

Let us say with Paul, when he spoke of the exceeding grace of God, "Thanks be to God for His indescribable gift!" (2 Corinthians 9:15).

∾Faith in Action∾

Express your faith in praise. Look up additional verses about God's grace. Compile a list of songs about grace, such as "Amazing Grace," "Grace Greater than Our Sin," "His Grace Reaches Me," and "Wonderful Grace of Jesus." In an hour of meditation, read the verses, sing the songs, and pray to God, thanking Him for His blessed gift of grace.

Apply Your Heart (Proverbs 2:2)

1. What are some ways people misunderstand or abuse God's grace? Do you have any personal examples that you are willing to share?

2. Paul referred to grace as "the free gift" (Romans 5:16). How is it free when the cost was so great (vv. 8, 9)?

3. What are the attributes of God listed in Deuteronomy 32:3, 4? How does this picture of God help us understand His matchless grace, and how we should respond to it?

4. What would you say to those who are involved in willful sin but excuse their actions by saying, "God's grace covers it"?

A Friend's Perspective

THEIR STORY: "My friend has been wayward since the beginning of 2010."

SCRIPTURES THEY'VE RELIED ON: Philippians 2:12; Proverbs 3:5, 6; James 1:2–4, 12; 1 Peter 5:7; 1 Chronicles 16:11

ADVICE THEY'D OFFER TO SOMEONE IN A SIMILAR SITUATION: "Obviously prayer should be your rock while you are dealing with this situation. The peace of God will help you deal with your feelings, dealing with them (helping you make the right decisions on how to help the situation), etc. Secondly, which I learned the hard way, was not to take their decision personally. Your first gut reaction (at least mine was) was that maybe I could have been there more, helped her more, done something different that would have made her not leave the Lord. It isn't your fault and their decision is against God, not you. 1 Pet. 5:8. After dealing with this for three years, I have come to the conclusion that you have to go on living YOUR life. Philippians 2:12. I know that that may sound selfish but for months after my friend left the Lord, it was all I could think about. It was on my mind constantly. It consumed me, my life, and my mind. I was so distraught over it that it was all I could think about. And I think that that would be one piece of advice that I would give someone dealing with this same situation. (I hope this makes sense and doesn't sound like I just gave up, because that is not the case at all)."

ADDITIONAL THOUGHTS: "At the present time, I do not hear from her much. I assume it is because she knows she is living in sin and doesn't want to have to talk to me. Even though we do not talk much at all, I still email her every month or so just to let her know I am still here if she ever needs someone to talk to (2 Thess. 3:13) if she ever wants to come back to the Lord. I think keeping in touch with them, even if you do not hear back from them, is very important. If they ever want to come back, they know they can still count on you to be there for them."

Chapter Nine

React in the Right Way

"REMEMBER THE LORD, GREAT AND AWESOME,
AND FIGHT FOR YOUR BRETHREN, YOUR SONS,
YOUR DAUGHTERS, YOUR WIVES, AND YOUR HOUSES."
NEHEMIAH 4:14

Recently I went to a new hairdresser. Imagine my delight when I learned she's a member of the church. She had just moved to Denver from Fort Worth that very week. I asked her which congregation she attended in Fort Worth. She said, "Oh, I actually quit going a while back and started attending a community church. My husband and I divorced and I felt very ... judged." I don't know her story. Perhaps it was an unscriptural divorce and the members tried to warn her. Or perhaps it was a scriptural divorce, but she was the guilty party. Did she repent, but felt the members treated her harshly? Or did she fail to repent and then felt judged by the members? Either way, one part reacted wrongly.

How are we to react when it's discovered that two members of the congregation have been engaged in a homosexual relationship? Or an adulterous relationship? How are we to react when we overhear a group of Christians discussing the latest unwholesome movie? Are we to be Church Police, cruising around and watching for someone to break the law of the Lord? Or are we to turn a blind eye, figuring it's none of our business? How do we react when learning that a loved one is engaged in willful sin? Let's make it a little more personal. How do YOU react when you find out a brother or sister has been lying to you? How do you react to your own sin? The real question is, how should you react?

Ezra was a scribe and priest. King Artaxerxes allowed Ezra to lead a group of Israelites back to Jerusalem. After being in Babylonian captivity, you can imagine how thrilling this was for them. The Lord blessed their journey with safety. They were given gold and silver to return to the temple. Everything was going well, until Ezra learned that the people, from the leaders down, committed a grievous sin against the Lord (Ezra 9:1, 2). Ezra was faced with the news that the people he cared about were guilty. As we study this text, we'll look at his reaction, God's reaction, and the sinners' reaction to a sinful situation.

Ezra's Reaction
He was deeply moved.

> *So when I heard this thing, I tore my garment and my robe, and plucked out some of the hair of my head and beard, and sat down astonished. (Ezra 9:3)*

Tearing of clothing was an expression of grief. Because Ezra tore his outer and inner garments, he was showing extreme grief. Shaving one's head or beard was common practice, but Ezra pulling out his hair was unique. Nehemiah pulled out hair, but it wasn't his own (Nehemiah 13:23–25). Nehemiah's reaction was one of indignation. Ezra's reaction was one of sorrow. He "sat astonished until the evening service" (9:3, 4). He sat there a long time, appalled. Sitting in silence was another sign of grief. Remember when Job's three friends visited? "They sat down with him on the ground seven days and seven nights, and no one spoke a word to him, for they saw that his grief was very great" (Job 2:13).

At the discovery of sin, Ezra was deeply moved. He certainly wasn't indifferent. Are we moved by sin? Do we grieve? Do we feel the shame? Christ does. When a Christian turns his back on the Lord, He is crucified all over again (Hebrews 6:6). That's the magnitude of sin. We need to make sure our hearts stay pure and tender so that we grieve when we hear of the sin-struggles of others.

He felt personally involved.

Read Ezra 9:4-6. Notice he felt the shame of the sinners, and he took ownership of the guilt. "**Our** iniquities have risen higher than our heads." Why? He was a spiritual leader, the priest. He involved himself. "Here we are before You, in our guilt" (v. 15). Ezra was told, "Arise, for this matter is your responsibility. We also are with you. Be of good courage, and do it" (10:4). It was time for Ezra to get up and take action. Taking action takes courage. Do we take responsibility? After all, we are spiritual leaders, aren't we? According to 1 Peter 2:9, we are a "royal priesthood." We take ownership by having the courage to take action.

He humbled himself.

The first thing to do is start praying, the get-down-on-your-knees kind of praying. Ezra prayed, confessed, wept, and bowed down before the house of God (10:1). He was lying outstretched on the ground with his face downward. He worshiped, fasted, and mourned "because of the guilt of those from the captivity" (v. 6). The guilt of the people really affected him. How could it be that a spiritual leader could maintain such a tender heart for the people? Their sin was what led them to captivity in the first place. What kept Ezra from just throwing his hands up in the air? The answer is found earlier in the book: "For Ezra had prepared his heart to seek the Law of the LORD, and to do it, and to teach statutes and ordinances in Israel" (7:10). He prepared his heart in two ways: to seek the law (diligent Bible study) and to do it (Bible living). "Then I proclaimed a fast there at the river of Ahava, that we might humble ourselves before our God, to seek from Him the right way for us and our little ones and all our possessions" (8:21). Ezra humbled himself to "seek from Him the right way." He prepared his heart and humbled himself. Because he knew the law, he revered it. It was in his heart. Because he humbled himself, he sought God's will.

Do you find yourself feeling indifferent to the sins of others? Do you find yourself impatient with those who struggle with sin? Have you given up on them? If so, maybe you have a heart problem. Prepare your heart and humble yourself.

Notice the effect Ezra's righteous reaction to sin had on the sinners (10:1, 2). The people came to him in tears! He didn't have to browbeat them or guilt trip them. They saw Ezra's commitment and righteousness and their consciences were pricked. They were ready to repent. Each individual is responsible for his or her own sin, but it's sobering to know that the condition of our hearts might effect how quickly another repents. We must prepare our hearts, and humble ourselves so that when faced with sin (whether the sins of others or our own), we will react in righteousness.

He didn't just react. He acted.

Ezra followed through with the hard part. He told the sinners, "You have transgressed" (10:10). He didn't try to make them feel better by excusing their sin. He didn't offer false comfort when he saw their bitter weeping. God doesn't want us to mislead sinners by assuring them they're okay (Jeremiah 23:17). Ezra also told them what they needed to do (10:11). Make confession, do God's will, and repent (undo the wrong). Ezra didn't ask anything of them he wasn't already doing himself.

God's Reaction
He was angry.

The people mentioned His "fierce wrath" (Ezra 10:14). We discussed God's holiness in the last chapter. Disobedience is not treating God as holy. Someone said, "Disobedience is a clenched fist and its object is the face of God." Does sin anger God today? Hebrews 10:26, 27 mentions God's "fiery indignation" when we sin willfully. It's possible to face the "wrath of God" (John 3:36). And Psalm 7:11 implies that God is angry at the wicked every day (see vv. 8, 9).

He was merciful.

God punished them less than they deserved (Ezra 9:13). This same verse mentions evil deeds, great guilt, and iniquity. Yet God was merciful. "For as the heavens are high above the earth, so great is His mercy toward those who fear Him" (Psalm 103:11). I'm thankful when I read, "For You, Lord, are good, and ready to forgive, and abundant in mercy to all those who call upon You" (86:5). God is rich in mercy (Ephesians 2:4)!

His righteousness was coupled with compassion.

God protected a remnant and allowed them in His presence (Ezra 9:15). Sometimes our so-called righteousness comes across as cold and judgmental. God is just and righteous AND compassionate.

> But He, being full of compassion, forgave their iniquity, and did not destroy them.
> Yes, many a time He turned His anger away, and did not stir up all His wrath.
> (Psalm 78:38)

He was gracious.

"And now for a little while grace has been shown from the LORD our God" (Ezra 9:8). Some say the God of the New Testament is a God of grace, but the God of the Old Testament was a God of retribution. That's just not true! God was full of grace from the beginning. "I am the LORD, I do not change" (Malachi 3:6). God has always offered grace and everlasting love to His people (Jeremiah 31:2, 3). Because of God's grace, He enlightened their eyes. They saw the error of their ways. Sin blinds. God extended grace by giving them revival in their bondage, an opportunity to go back to Jerusalem, and an opportunity to leave the slavery of sin. And God was gracious by delivering them (Ezra 9:13).

What do we learn from God's reaction? His mercy, compassion, and grace led Him to help His people see their sin, to offer hope, and to help them find a way out. And God is the very One they sinned against. He did not forsake them; He extended mercy. He helped them revive, repair, and rebuild.

The Sinners' Reaction

Have you ever been caught up in a sin? Maybe what used to be an occasional slip-up has become a bad habit. Maybe you find yourself enjoying a particular sin too much and can't seem to resist the pleasure it offers. There are many temptations facing us—gossip, impure speech, jealousy, reading or viewing sensual material. What if a friendly relationship with someone of the opposite sex, even a fellow Christian, has turned flirtatious? You realize you're playing with fire, but it's too thrilling and exciting. Surely it won't lead to anything more serious. Have you ever been caught up in sin? Was that sin ever exposed? If so, how did you react when your guilt came to light? Or maybe you're currently struggling with a hidden sin. None of us are immune. Are your eyes open to the magnitude of it? Are you treating God as holy? Let's look at the sinners' reaction in Ezra.

Their hearts were pricked.

They "wept very bitterly" (Ezra 10:1). Their consciences weren't dull. The more we pursue sin, the more our hearts aren't bruised by it.

When we live with hypocrisy, when we lie to others and even ourselves, we sear our consciences with a hot iron (1 Timothy 4:2). That means the conscience is cauterized, no longer able to feel the pain that alerts it to danger. Practically speaking, as we pursue sin, we lose the power of moral decision-making.

The conscience can be defiled (Titus 1:15). Paul said we're either living pure lives or defiled lives. When we toy with things that aren't pure, we become defiled. There's no such thing as a pure person dabbling in unrighteousness.

The sinners of Ezra's day reacted with bitter tears when faced with their sin. They didn't get mad. Hugh Troyer said, "I have known many people that do things they know are wrong. Then when someone that cares about them tries to talk to them about the problem, they get mad about it. Always remember this—when you do something that you know is wrong, you give up the right to get mad."

They sought out a spiritual leader.

The people gathered around Ezra because they saw his heart (10:1). They knew he was committed to God, and they knew he cared. They didn't try to figure things out on their own. They sought help. They trusted their spiritual leader. God designed His body to have spiritual leaders. Our elders are charged with warning the unruly, comforting the faint-hearted, and upholding the weak (1 Thessalonians 5:14). They want us to go to them when we're struggling.

They confessed their sin.

What was the first thing they said to Ezra? "We have trespassed against our God" (10:2). They didn't minimize their sin or rename it. They owned up to it. They even confessed how they specifically sinned against God: "[We] have taken pagan wives from the peoples of the land." Notice what's missing? Excuses. Justification. Blame. If we get caught up in sin, we need to own up to it. We're not treating God as holy. We need to confess our sin without trying to soften or excuse it, without blaming circumstances or spouse or church.

They repented.

Their repentance involved undoing the wrong they had done (Ezra 10:3). They vowed to put away their foreign (unscriptural) wives. Think how difficult that must've been! And yet, one by one, they repented. No one was excused. Even the sons of the priests promised to put away their wives and offer a ram as a sin offering.

Some are confused about the idea of repentance. It's not enough to grieve for sin, even to feel horrible. If we don't repent by changing our ways, giving up the sin, and undoing the wrong to the best of our ability, then we still carry the weight of the guilt. Sorrow plus correction equals repentance (Ezra 10:12–14). Someone said, "Sin forsaken is the best evidence of sin forgiven." Paul wrote, "Godly sorrow produces repentance leading to salvation" (2 Corinthians 7:10).

If we find ourselves caught up in sin, we need to act while our hearts are still tender before the conscience is defiled. Someone said, "The longer you delay, the more your sin gets strength and rooting. If you cannot bend a twig, how will you be able to bend it when it is a tree?" We have the blessing of being able to go to our spiritual leaders for guidance and prayer. Then it is up to us to confess and repent.

Both Ezra and the sinners acknowledged their sin (9:10), God's mercy (v. 13), their need of repentance and not doing it again (v. 14), God's goodness (v. 15), their hope (10:2), and the action they had to take (v. 3). When we acknowledge our sin and repent, God in His goodness offers mercy and hope. How we react to sin, whether our own or the sins of others, has eternal consequences.

∾Faith in Action∾

Start cultivating a heart like Ezra's. Notice how many times he praised God and prayed to God. He credited God for every good thing, and he prayed to God in every situation. Using two different colors, underline Ezra's praises and prayers. Praises: 7:27, 28; 8:18, 22, 31. Prayers: 8:21, 23; 9:5; 10:1.

Apply Your Heart (Proverbs 2:2)

1. According to the following verses, what happens when we confess our sins?

» 1 John 1:9 _____

» James 5:16 _____

2. What did genuine repentance yield in 2 Corinthians 7:11? How did it influence Paul's feelings toward the church at Corinth (v. 16)?

3. Read Artaxerxes' letter to Ezra (Ezra 7:12–26). How many times did Artaxerxes mention God? Do you think Artaxerxes knew Ezra had prepared his heart to serve God?

4. The Righteous Reaction to Sin

    a.   List the "-ed" words in Ezra 9:4-6.

    b.   List the "-ing" words in Ezra 10:1.

A Father's Perspective

HIS STORY: "My daughter has been wayward and in a lesbian relationship since 1999."

ADVICE HE'D OFFER TO SOMEONE IN A SIMILAR SITUATION: "Parents should discuss these issues with their children. Homosexuality is so common today that it's easy for parents to have those conversations with their children. Had we discussed this issue with our daughter during her childhood, maybe things would have been different."

ADDITIONAL THOUGHTS: "I don't know how God is going to hold parents accountable for their children's actions, and this is not just a dodge or a cop-out on my part. I'm surely not meaning to be disrespectful to God, but He made only two people—His children, and they became unfaithful. What did He do wrong? I know that Scripture teaches us to train our children, but at what point does the child become a responsible person and relieve the parents from being responsible for their children's actions? I don't want to appear heartless, but I don't have a 'Messiah Complex' in which I believe that I can save everyone, even my own children. I do what I can to save everyone and leave the rest to them, to others, and to God. It grieves me that [my daughter] is not faithful, but I can't let her actions take away the joy of my salvation."

Chapter Ten

Keep Your Cup Filled

"MY SOUL MELTS FROM HEAVINESS;
STRENGTHEN ME ACCORDING TO YOUR WORD."
PSALM 119:28

After enjoying a great lectureship or gospel meeting, we often say something like, "My cup is full!" We mean that we've been so uplifted or challenged by the lessons and fellowship that we feel spiritually filled to the brim.

David relied on God to fill his cup. In Psalm 23, there are twelve references to God, seventeen personal pronouns, and fourteen blessings. David was personally blessed by God's guidance, protection, comfort, and hospitality. He said, "My cup runs over." Scholars explain that the cup is often used figuratively to represent the "condition of life, prosperous or miserable."[1]

Would you describe your life's condition as prosperous or miserable? David knew how to keep his cup filled, prosperous, and overflowing, and we can do the same.

How to Drink in God's Goodness

David completely relied on God to sustain him. He acknowledged God's hand in his life, from basic physical necessities to spiritual fulfillment. God's goodness is abundant, as evidenced by His daily blessings. Sometimes we simply need to acknowledge them and soak them in.

---

1 M. Unger, *The New Unger's Bible Dictionary* (Chicago: Moody, 1988).

From Psalm 23, we see several ways we can allow God to fill our cups.

Trust in God's providence.

"The LORD is my shepherd; I shall not want" (Psalm 23:1). In this psalm, David compared his relationship with God to that of a sheep with its shepherd. Having been a shepherd boy (1 Samuel 17:15, 20, 34), David understood very well the trust-and-obey relationship sheep have with their shepherd. Sheep are utterly dependent upon their shepherd. The first blessing David acknowledged is that with God as our Shepherd, all of our needs will be supplied. Are you trying to rely on yourself? If so, aren't you tired of that? Jesus assured us, "I am the good shepherd; and I know My sheep" (John 10:14). He knows us better than we know ourselves; therefore, He knows our needs better than we do. If we trust in ourselves to take care of our needs, we will find that something is missing. What a blessing to trust in God, knowing He will think of everything!

Relax in God's protection.

"He makes me to lie down in green pastures" (Psalm 23:2). Sheep will not lie down when afraid. God protects His own. We can feel secure in His care. He knows where the green pastures are, and He wants us to look to Him for protection. How much does God desire to protect us? Enough that He was willing to lay down His life for us. "I am the good shepherd. The good shepherd gives His life for the sheep. But a hireling, he who is not the shepherd, one who does not own the sheep, sees the wolf coming and leaves the sheep and flees; and the wolf catches the sheep and scatters them. The hireling flees because he is a hireling and does not care about the sheep" (John 10:11–13). Because God cares about us, we are safe in Him.

Rely on God's guidance.

"He leads me beside the still waters" (Psalm 23:2b). From what I understand, sheep won't drink from rushing waters. If we let Him, God will lead us to the still waters. When I think of rushing water, I think of turbulence. That is what we will find when we refuse to rely on God's guidance.

Rest in God's restoration.

"He restores my soul" (Psalm 23:3). This is what we all crave. When we're weary of worries and cares, our souls desire to be made whole again—to be returned to the peace we once had and the joy we felt. David reminded us that God offers that for us, and he knew that from personal experience (Psalm 51, particularly v. 12).

Follow God's direction.

"He leads me in the paths of righteousness for His name's sake" (Psalm 23:3b). We already know the righteous path is narrow and difficult (Matthew 7:13, 14). God wants to guide us. If we follow Him, we will stay on the right path. "He calls his own sheep by name and leads them out. And when he brings out his own sheep, he goes before them; and the sheep follow him, for they know his voice" (John 10:3, 4). Somewhere along the way, our wayward loved ones quit following God's direction, and so strayed off course. We must stay the course, not only for our sake but also for when our loved ones are ready to return to the straight and narrow! For a personal refresher on how to stay the course, read Psalm 119:1–8.

Remember God's presence.

"Yea, though I walk through the valley of the shadow of death, I will fear no evil; for You are with me" (Psalm 23:4). It's hard to feel empty when mindful of God's abiding presence. We mustn't let Satan trick us into thinking God has forsaken us. He never will (Hebrews 13:5). And remember, this promise is from One who can never break a promise! I rejoice when I sing the words to an old hymn by L. O. Sanderson.

The Lord Has Been Mindful of Me

By L. O. Sanderson

Though I, thro' the valley of shadow,
O'er mountain or troubled sea,
And oft in the darkness have travelled,

The Lord has been mindful of me!

Much more than my grief and my sorrow,
Much more than adversity,
Much more than the all I have given,
The Lord has been mindful of me!

The Lord has been mindful of me!
He blesses and blesses again!
My God is the God of the living!
How excellent is His name!

Take comfort in God's involvement.

"Your rod and Your staff, they comfort me" (Psalm 23:4b). According to Matthew Henry's commentary, this verse is "alluding to the shepherd's crook, or the rod under which the sheep passed when they were counted (Leviticus 27:32), or the staff with which the shepherds drove away the dogs that would scatter or worry the sheep."[1] The rod and staff were the shepherd's tools, which he used for guidance and protection. The shepherd kept track of his sheep, kept danger away from his sheep, and at times, disciplined his sheep. It's comforting to know that our Shepherd is that involved in our lives today. He knows us, protects us, and, at times, uses the rod to discipline us for our own good (Hebrews 12:5–11).

Look for God's sanctuary.

"You prepare a table before me in the presence of my enemies" (Psalm 23:5). The last two verses of Psalm 23 picture God as the hospitable host. David found sanctuary in the many ways we've already seen, which culminated in God's house. He found security even in the presence of his enemies. He found his needs met in God's providence of the table. We could even say David found restoration, as God clearly showed the ene-

---

1 M. Henry, "Ps. 23:1–6," *Mathew Henry's Commentary on the Whole Bible: Complete and Unabridged in One Volume* (Peabody: Hendrickson, 1996).

mies His favor toward David. There is sanctuary for us in God's house! Our enemy, Satan, isn't just going after our loved ones; he wants us, too. But as long as we remain in God's house, Satan can't touch us. Paul explained that the household of God is the church and described it as the "pillar and ground of the truth" (1 Timothy 3:15). Some versions read "buttress," which is a defense or support. There is safety in God's house. That is where we find sanctuary against the enemy, against those who do not understand our stand for the truth (even when it involves family).

Rejoice in God's generosity.

"You anoint my head with oil; my cup runs over" (Psalm 23:5b). Here we see God's generosity as host. According to *Easton's Bible Dictionary*, olive oil was a valuable product, and the "use of it was a sign of gladness (Psalm 92:10; Isaiah 61:3)."[1] Offering oil to a guest was a thoughtful, courteous thing to do, showing the host's willingness to consider and meet every need.

The overflowing cup also speaks of God's generosity. According to scholars, this is the only time the word for "runs over" or "overflows" appears in the Old Testament.[2] I sat in a class once where the teacher explained that the Hebrew host would keep filling the cup as long as he wanted his guest to stay. When he let the cup run dry, he was informing the guest that it was time to go. If this is the case, then we are always welcome in God's house because our cup overflows (which would tie in to the last phrase of this psalm). Or it could be that David was describing his host as providing more than enough. Either way we see God's generosity toward those in His house.

Cling to God's promises.

"Surely goodness and mercy shall follow me all the days of my life; and I will dwell in the house of the LORD forever" (Psalm 23:6). David is confident in two things: God's providence and God's acceptance. God's

---

1 M.G. Easton, *Easton's Bible Dictionary* (Oak Harbor: Logos Research Systems, 1996).

2 R.G. Bratcher and W.D. Reyburn, "Helps for Translators," *A Translator's Handbook on the Book of Psalms* (New York: United Bible Societies, 1991), 235.

providence is seen in His goodness and mercy (or lovingkindness), and God's acceptance is seen in David abiding in His house. Notice their duration. David said "all the days of my life" and "forever." No matter if he walked through the valley or faced the enemy, David relied on the promises of God to carry him through this life, and the next. Let's remember to drink in God's goodness!

How to Drink in God's Goodness

What can we do on a daily basis to make sure our cups stay full? Here are several practical ideas:

Do for Others

In the Old and New Testament, God said He would bless us when we bless others (Isaiah 58:10, 11; Matthew 25:34–40). Even though the following ideas might take a little time and effort, we should remember that the giver often ends up feeling happy and whole.

Try to make visits (to the hospital or to shut-ins) at least once a month. Take muffins or flowers, keep it brief, and offer to pray (if appropriate). Even better, ask a teenage girl or single woman to go with you.

Offer to babysit for a young family so the parents can have a date night. Offer to "parent-sit" for a couple who is caring for a dependent parent in their home so they can have a date night.

Visit your local safe houses and find practical ways to help. Women needing refuge from domestic violence are seeking security and genuine love!

Take Advantage of Christian Fellowship

Some people just really don't enjoy potlucks. If you're one of those people, go anyway. It's really all about fellowship, spending time with the saints, getting into one another's lives, and encouraging others.

Have folks into your home once a month. If you're having your peers over, make sure you also invite someone you don't know very well. If you're young, have the elderly over. If you're older, have the young folks into your home. It doesn't have to be an elaborate meal; it's all about tearing down personal walls and building relationships.

Get involved in or start service and benevolent projects with fellow saints.

Deepen Your Bible Study

Go as deep as you can, challenging yourself with something new to study. Start Bible-marking specific topics. If you're unfamiliar with Bible-marking, go to www.life-and-favor.com and search "Bible-marking." The one about "Marriage Builders from Proverbs" also includes instructions about how to do it. You'll find additional Bible-marking exercises, with topics relating to the subject of this book, provided as an appendix. Use these as an aide throughout this study. Start color-coding key words in each book of the Bible. Grow closer to Jesus by going through each of the Gospels and learning from Him. How does He handle conflict? What emotions does He display? How did He spend His time?

Think Souls

If you're nervous about having an open Bible study with someone, sign up to help with Bible Correspondence Courses. Go on a short-term mission trip. Save up for it or raise support. Ask a soul-winner to include you in their next study.

If you're already involved in Bible studies, invite one of the teens to join you on your next one. Help create an evangelistic-minded congregation by talking about it, praying about it, and looking for ways to keep the momentum going.

Go through your church directory and pray for one family each day.

Perform Secret Acts of Kindness

Everyone loves surprises. Send small gifts (chocolate, note cards, fruit, lotion, pens) for no reason to those who will least expect it. Shovel or rake your neighbor's yard. Send flowers (or something else she'd enjoy) to your church secretary.

Mail encouraging notes to your elders, telling them what a great job they are doing. If you can afford it, secretly send a restaurant gift card to a young couple.

Take Advantage of Inspirational Sources

There are several Christian websites available for those who would like a spiritual boost. A couple that include Bible-marking topics are

» *Come Fill Your Cup* is written by women and for women. It has new articles available nearly every day and also includes in-depth Bible studies. Visit: *comefillyourcup.com.*

» *Life and Favor* is my blog. It contains articles about Christian living, Bible-marking, and interviews of Christian women. Visit: *life-and-favor.com.*

» *Christian Courier* is a comprehensive Bible study web site that contains sound articles on a wide variety of topics. Visit: *ChristianCourier.com.*

Renew your subscription to uplifting periodicals like *Christian Woman.* Build your spiritual literature library by ordering the latest books written by Christians. Try to fit in at least one lectureship or seminar each year.

Opportunities to enjoy the blessings of God's goodness are all around us! When praying for, pleading with, and persuading a wayward loved one to come back home, we can find ourselves tapped out if we're not careful. Let's keep our cups full by acknowledging God's goodness and looking for ways to practically enjoy them.

⌒Faith in Action⌒

Choose one of the practical ways to drink in God's goodness mentioned in this chapter and put it into practice this week.

Apply Your Heart (Proverbs 2:2)

1. Turn to Isaiah 58:10, 11.

    a.   What two things are we supposed to be doing for others?

    b.   What are some practical ways we can accomplish those two things?

    c.   What seven blessings are ours when we do those two things?

2. According to Isaiah 32:17–18, what is the work of righteousness? What is the effect of righteousness? How does this help us keep our cups full?

3. What can we learn of God's goodness from the following verses?

    a.   Isaiah 43:2

    b.   Psalm 3

    c.   Psalm 27:1

    d.   Psalm 16:5–8

4. Turn to Psalm 23. If you like to mark your Bible, draw a square around each reference to God. Circle each personal pronoun. And underline each listed blessing.

A Best Friend's Perspective

THEIR STORY: "My best friend has been wayward for eight or nine years."

SCRIPTURES THEY'VE RELIED ON: James 5:19, 20

ADVICE THEY'D OFFER TO SOMEONE IN A SIMILAR SITUATION: "Do not be afraid to say something early on. Most don't just fall away over night. It is a long process. My regret is that by the time I said anything it was too late."

ADDITIONAL THOUGHTS: "It pretty much ended our friendship. We are still friendly when we talk; we just don't talk much."

Chapter Eleven

Protect Your Family

"SHE WATCHES OVER THE WAYS OF HER HOUSEHOLD, AND DOES
NOT EAT THE BREAD OF IDLENESS. HER CHILDREN RISE UP AND
CALL HER BLESSED; HER HUSBAND ALSO, AND HE PRAISES HER."
PROVERBS 31:27, 28

Nicole's dad committed adultery and then divorced her mom in order to be with the other woman. Soon after, Nicole's mom turned away from God in anger and bitterness. As Nicole struggled to grasp the fact that her parents had turned into strangers, she found herself floundering spiritually. She lost interest in her friends and the activities that used to bring her joy. She even found that taking care of her husband and small children took more effort than she felt she could give. While Nicole is a made-up name, the story is true. In addition to remaining strong spiritually, emotionally, and physically when a loved one falls away, we also need to make sure our families remain strong in those same areas. The last thing we need to do is add the burden of guilt when we already feel weighed down. While a certain amount of grieving is unavoidable when a loved one falls away, there are things we can do to make sure we're not hurting our own families in the process.

Reign in Your Emotions

Nicole found that she couldn't stop crying. Month after month she went through boxes of tissue. Songs in worship, family pictures, questions from others, or a sympathetic look from her husband all set her off. She didn't know it was physically possible to produce that many tears. Unfortunately, her young children began to fear their mother would never be the same again. And her husband felt like he had to fill in the gap when his wife was too distracted to be the mother their children needed.

Children need stability. Seeing their mom cry so often creates anxiety. A certain amount of weeping is normal, but an excessive prolonging of grief or worry will eventually take its toll on the rest of the family. If you find yourself unable to focus on the needs of your family because your despair is so great, it might be time to seek help. Long periods of stress or grief can turn into clinical depression. Take care of yourself so you can take care of the family relying on you.

Invest Time in Your Family

It took Nicole a long time before she realized her family was suffering. She'd been blind to their needs. Looking back, she feels like she lost an entire year with them. Her children's milestones from that year are only foggy memories.

You've spent time praying for and pleading with your wayward loved one. Don't neglect to spend time each day with your spouse and your children. They're hurting, too. Read to your children. Go for a walk with your spouse. Talk about God's blessings, and share the things you appreciate about your family with your family. Instead of agonizing over the vacant chair at family gatherings, try to focus on the ones who are present. Let the wayward know you miss them, but make sure the ones you're with know you treasure them. Not only will spending time with your family reassure them, but it will strengthen you. It will remind you of the responsibilities and blessings you still have.

Spare Them the Details

Because Nicole's dad tried to justify his actions, he spilled all the nitty-gritty details of his thirty years of marriage. Because Nicole's mom was hurt, she revealed to her daughter all the times that her dad messed up.

Nicole ended up feeling like her entire upbringing was a farce. She carried the unhappy knowledge of every lie and betrayal in her parents' marriage and didn't know what to do with it. It broke her heart, and she resented both of her parents for making her the unwilling recipient of their painful secrets.

Use wisdom when deciding how much to share with your family. Spare your children as much of the pain as you can by sparing them the gruesome details, if there are any. We might feel as if unloading the entire story will be cathartic, but if we're not careful, we could do more harm than good.

Solomon reminded us of the importance of wisdom and discretion in this very situation:

When wisdom enters your heart, and knowledge is pleasant to your soul, discretion will preserve you; understanding will keep you, to deliver you from the way of evil, from the man who speaks perverse things, from those who leave the paths of uprightness to walk in the ways of darkness. (Proverbs 2:10–13)

When trying to determine just how much to share, consider some simple questions:

1. Is the information age appropriate? Are your children too young to fully understand the nature of what you're sharing?

2. How will sharing the details impact relationships if/ when the wayward decides to repent and return?

3. Will sharing certain details damage precious memories?

4. Will it cause regret later on your part?

5. Will the details cause bitterness, discouragement, or doubt?

While these may seem like no-brainers, it's still good to be reminded to stop and think before speaking. When caught up in the very real drama of something as painful as a loved one falling away, we might find it more difficult to continue to think rationally. However, in order to protect our precious families, it's important that we do so.

Help Them See the Spiritual Lessons

While younger children don't need to know all the details, there are things they will know no matter what. They will see for themselves the spiritual decline of their relative (parent, sibling, aunt, uncle). They will see them missing worship and avoiding family gatherings. They might notice a change in their demeanor, such as in their personality or speech. They might hear them speak belligerently about God, the church, their family, rules, expectations, hypocrisies, etc. Your children now have, unfortunately, a living example of apostasy. And since you don't want them to follow in that example, you must help them learn from their loved one's mistakes.

Spiritual Lesson #1: Choices Have Consequences

In hindsight, we often can see how a series of unwise choices led to unhappy circumstances. If that is the case with your wayward loved one, you can help your children see the impact of their decisions.

Did they marry a non-Christian who made it difficult for them to remain faithful? Did they surround themselves with worldly influences? Did they seem to have a hard time submitting to biblical authority? Did they choose a career path that kept them away from worship? Did they experiment with a sinful practice and then get caught in its web? If there is a clear reason why your loved one fell away, help your children see it so they will learn from it.

Some scriptures to study with your children concerning choices and consequences:

- » Deuteronomy 30:9–20
- » Proverbs 3:1–35; 14:12
- » Galatians 6:7, 8
- » Colossians 3:17
- » James 4:4

Some Bible characters to study who suffered consequences for their choices:

» Adam and Eve (Genesis 3)
» Lot (Genesis 13:10, 11; 19:1–30)
» Moses (Numbers 20:1–12)
» David (2 Samuel 11–12)

Spiritual Lesson #2: No One Is Immune from Temptation

There are times when no one is surprised when a certain person leaves the Lord. Perhaps that person had a tendency to flirt with danger or rebel against authority.

But sometimes, everyone is surprised when a certain person leaves the Lord. Perhaps that person was a seemingly strong and faithful Christian who looked like they were doing everything right. Everyone is left asking, "What happened?"

Remind your children of the persistent Satan, who walks about like a roaring lion, seeking someone to devour (1 Peter 5:8). Satan is real. Temptation is real. And we must remember to arm ourselves against it, no matter who we are.

Scriptures to study with your children about temptation:

» Romans 3:23
» 1 Corinthians 10:13
» Ephesians 6:10–18
» James 1:12–15; 4:7

Bible characters to study of good men who were tempted:

» Job (Job 1:1–2:10)
» Joseph (Genesis 39:6–12)
» Jesus (Luke 4:1–13)

Spiritual Lesson #3: Faith Must Be Real and Personal

Some young adults fall away when they leave home because they have yet to own their faith. Some older adults fall away when they face trials because they have yet to mature their faith. What could be more important than impressing upon our children the essentiality of genuine, personal faith? It's what will carry them through the storms of life. It's what will ground them when truth is attacked. It's what will guide them when the world presses close.

Oh how important it is to help our children develop their own personal relationship with the Father! We must study with them so they'll know how. We must encourage them so they won't forget. And we must pray with them so they'll trust in their Lord.

Scriptures to study with your children about real faith:

> » Romans 10:17
> » 2 Corinthians 13:5
> » Hebrews 11
> » James 2:19–26
> » 1 Peter 1:3–9

Bible characters to study whose faith carried them through trials:

> » Abraham (Genesis 22:1–18; Hebrews 11:17–19)
> » Shadrach, Meshach, and Abed-Nego (Daniel 3)
> » Daniel (Daniel 6)
> » Paul (Acts 21:8–14)

∽Faith in Action∾

Make sure your immediate family is strengthening themselves spiritually. Focus devotional talks toward the spiritual lessons mentioned in this chapter. Introduce faith-building topics into your conversations as often as possible.

Apply Your Heart (Proverbs 2:2)

1. The "whole armor of God" is our defense against "the wiles of the devil" (Ephesians 6:11). Beside each word below, list a practical way to "wear it" or put it into practice.

    a.   Truth

    b.   Righteousness

    c.   Peace

    d.   Faith

    e.   Salvation

    f.   Word of God

    g.   Prayer

2. Think of additional Bible characters whose choices carried heavy consequences. What could/should they have done differently?

3. Think of additional Bible characters whose faith was tested. When they were faithful to God, was He faithful to them?

4. Write Proverbs 15:2 in your own words. How does this passage apply to the idea of protecting our families?

A Daughter's Perspective

HER STORY: "My father has been wayward for twelve years."

SCRIPTURES SHE'S RELIED ON: Psalm 33:13–15; 34:17–19; 56:1–13; 2 Corinthians 1:3, 4

ADVICE SHE'D OFFER TO SOMEONE IN A SIMILAR SITUATION: "Do whatever you can to feed your own soul. While my earthly father let me down, I had to grasp the truth that my heavenly Father never will. Satan wants us to doubt. We must fortify our faith continually with God's Word. His love protects and enables us; His church strengthens and nourishes us."

ADDITIONAL THOUGHTS: "I take comfort in the knowledge that even if my dad isn't interested in listening to me, God always listens. I know that as long as I keep talking to God, I won't drift away from Him in discouragement. I also take comfort in the fact that God knows what to do with my anger. I can cast every care on Him (1 Peter 5:7)."

Chapter Twelve

Don't Give Up,
but Know When to Let Go

"CASTING ALL YOUR CARE UPON HIM,
FOR HE CARES FOR YOU."
1 PETER 5:7

"CAST YOUR BURDEN ON THE LORD,
AND HE SHALL SUSTAIN YOU."
PSALM 55:22

H as it been months or even years since your loved one fell away, and you've tried everything? You've prayed. You've pleaded. You've shared God's Word. You've told them your heart is breaking. You've told them you're worried about their soul, that now you fear judgment because you know they're not ready to face that day. Nothing you've said or done has seemed to faze them. Even worse, they resent you for reaching out to them. Now what? What can you say that you haven't said? What can you pray that you haven't prayed? It could be that it's time to let go.

Since letting go is one of those things that's easier said than done, the purpose of this chapter will be to discuss how to let go. How can we continue on with our lives in such a way that we're able to enjoy the riches of our own relationship with God? How can we let go of the anxious need to think of something to say or do that will bring our loved ones back?

Turn It Over to God

You might be thinking, "I have been!" Maybe, though, it's time to turn it over to God completely. I'll never forget a sermon my dad preached many years ago about worry. He quoted 1 Peter 5:7: "Casting all your care upon Him, for He cares for you." He said our problem is that we treat it like we're fishing. We cast it all on Him, but then we reel it right back in.

First Peter 5:7 is sandwiched between two verses telling us to be humble and be sober. We're to be humble so God can exalt us. We're to be sober because Satan is after us. And in the middle of that, we're to cast all our cares upon God. Notice what ties these three thoughts together. Verse 1 mentions "the sufferings of Christ." Verse 9 mentions "the same sufferings are experienced by your brotherhood in the world." And then verse 10 says, "after you have suffered a while." The context of 1 Peter 5:7 is suffering! Sometimes suffering is a result of living right (see 3:17). That's what we're experiencing as we reach out to wayward loved ones. It would be a lot easier to give in to their choices or lifestyle, to reject God's teachings about sin, or to act like nothing's wrong. It would smooth our relationships and restore harmony in our families. But no, we want to be right, do right, live right. Being right in God's eyes means we'll oppose anything that is wrong in God's eyes—even when the wrong is committed by those dearest to us. And so, it can be hard and painful. We can suffer for it. What can we do? Be humble. Turn it over to God. Be sober.

If we do those three things during suffering, something beautiful happens. Look at 1 Peter 5:10: "But may the God of all grace, who called us to His eternal glory by Christ Jesus, after you have suffered a while, perfect, establish, strengthen, and settle you." Let's take a closer look at these four things God can do for us when we turn our pain over to Him.

- » Perfect (*katartizo*) — to restore; prepare
- » Establish (*sterizo*) — to set up; establish
- » Strengthen (*sthenoo*) — to strengthen; make more able
- » Settle (*themelioo*) — to lay a foundation[1]

---

1 G. Kittel, G. Friedrich, and G.W. Bromily, eds., *Theological Dictionary of the New Testament* (Grand Rapids: Eerdmans, 1995), 322.

As you look at what those words mean in the original language, don't you crave ALL of them as you're trying to continue to do the right thing? As wonderful as that is, the beautiful part is knowing the verb tense of these four words. They are indicative. What does that mean exactly? It means "the mood in which the action of the verb or the state of being it describes is presented by the writer as real. It is the mood of assertion, where the writer portrays something as actual (as opposed to possible or contingent on intention)."[1] In other words, these are not just hopeful possibilities. They are promises! If we cast all our cares upon the Lord during suffering, He WILL perfect us. He WILL establish us. He WILL strengthen us. And He WILL settle us. Restoration. Capability. Security. Only God can grant us these things as we turn our wayward loved ones over to Him.

Reclaim Your Peace

Remember Philippians 4:6, 7? "Be anxious for nothing, but in everything by prayer and supplication, with thanksgiving, let your requests be made known to God; and the peace of God, which surpasses all understanding, will guard your hearts and minds through Christ Jesus." When we turn everything over to God, His peace guards our hearts and minds.

Reclaiming peace involves trusting God. We will trust Him to keep our hearts untroubled and unafraid. Jesus said, "Peace I leave with you, My peace I give to you; not as the world gives do I give to you. Let not your heart be troubled, neither let it be afraid" (John 14:27). This was the second time Jesus said to His apostles, "Let not your heart be troubled" (see v. 1). They were perplexed. They had some concerns and questions (13:25, 36, 37; 14:5, 22). Jesus wanted them to know that even though the task facing them was great, He would take care of them and they could have peace. Even if our loved ones never repent (God forbid!), we will trust God with our hearts. Only in this way can we enjoy His peace.

---

1 H.S. Heiser, *Glossary of Morpho-Syntactic Database Terminology*, Logos Bible Software, 2005.

Remember, God Loves Them Even More Than You Do

This fact brings great assurance. As much as we love our dear ones and fear for their souls, our love can't compare to the vast love of their Father. He wants them to spend eternity with Him, even though they have rejected Him. God has all the power and wisdom. He knows all the details. He knows what's best for them. And He really cares. Because of this, we can let go. We can safely turn our loved ones over to the One who gave everything for them (1 John 4:9, 10).

Where to Go from Here

Turning it over to God doesn't mean you will stop trying to reach out to your wayward loved ones. So here are some practical ways to proceed:

1. Continue to pray for them.

2. Make sure they know you haven't given up on them. When you see them, tell them you're still praying and always will.

3. Tell God you trust Him with your loved one and with your heart. Then prove it by taking a deep breath and trying to release the burden.

4. Study Hebrews 6:4–6. While an initial reading may seem discouraging, as if it's impossible for the wayward to return, the text actually teaches that WE can't make someone return. WE can't "renew them again to repentance." It's a choice they have to make for themselves. The reason is given in verse 6: "Since they crucify again for themselves the Son of God, and put Him to an open shame."

5. Make sure you're living right. As mentioned in previous chapters, we must guard our own souls. John Broger said, "You can never truly understand or help others, even in your own family, unless you first look thoroughly into your own life and deal with your own sins without compromise, excuses, or evasions."

6. Focus on enjoying God's daily blessings. Not only will this bring you peace, but it will be noticed by others, including your wayward loved ones who might then remember what they are missing.

Staying True

By Kathy Pollard

I used to walk hand in hand
with those who guided me along the narrow way.
The path seemed smooth, life seemed bright
as we journeyed day to day.

Then the ones whose counsel I had sought
stumbled and fell in the sand.
I turned around to help them up.
They rejected my outstretched hand.

They wandered off into the dark.
Their new way was wide and broad.
I couldn't understand why they left me,
why they turned away from God.

Should I leave the path to look for them,
or in despair sit down and wait?
No, I'll stay the course and shine the Light,
so they can find their way back before it's too late.

～Faith in Action～

Look at the "Where to Go from Here" list. Do #'s 3 and 4 before the day ends. How can you daily and tangibly put #6 into practice? Write down at least a week's worth of ideas.

Apply Your Heart (Proverbs 2:2)

1. I once heard that Psalm 119 is the longest chapter, Psalm 117 is the shortest chapter, and Psalm 118 is the middle chapter of the Bible. In this middle chapter of the Bible, there are at least 10 verses that can encourage us as we turn our loved ones over to the Lord. See if you can find them.

2. Fear feeds fear. Is trust also contagious? Read Psalm 40:1–3 and discuss what happens when we trust God in difficult situations.

3. Write down the four things Paul encouraged the Corinthians to do in 1 Corinthians 16:13.

 a. _____

 b. _____

 c. _____

 d. _____

4. What's the hardest aspect of turning your wayward loved one over to God?

A Grandmother's Perspective

Her story: "My son and grown grandson have both been out of duty for about five years."

Scriptures she's relied on: "Proverbs 22:6. I know there are exceptions to this, but I do know that my son was taught from the time he was born. Hebrews 10:25. I keep sending this scripture to them hoping it will make them think. First John 5:15. I believe they must change their hearts, so I just pray that God will open their hearts to return before it is too late."

Advice she'd offer to someone in a similar situation: "I believe we can be too pushy and cause them to back off or, worse, not want to be around us by always bringing up the subject of them not coming to church. We should use every opportunity to show them we love them, no matter what they have done."

Additional thoughts: "NEVER, NEVER give up asking God to open their hearts. I also write them an email about every two to three months, encouraging them to consider the alternative, if they do not return ... . The last time I wrote to them, I told them to remember that hell is for eternity, just like heaven, and asked them to please read the story of the rich man and Lazarus. I never get an answer, but I do know they read it."

Chapter Thirteen

Learn from the Ones Who Came Back

"FOR YOUR BROTHER WAS DEAD AND IS ALIVE AGAIN,
AND WAS LOST AND IS FOUND."
LUKE 15:32

You probably know more former prodigals than you think you do. In preparing to write this final chapter, I asked to hear from Christians who were wayward at some point in their lives but had come back home. I was amazed at the response and very surprised by some whom I'd never guessed had been wayward. There were Christians who'd left the Lord for as long as twenty-five years, but who are now stronger than ever. That's encouraging! It offers hope for those who have loved ones who have fallen away. The thoughts shared by the returned prodigals are worth considering. They've been there. They know what it's like to wander away. More importantly, something made them come back home. I'm grateful to them for being willing to share their personal thoughts with us. Their insight can help us as we reach out to our own prodigals.

What We Can Learn

The passing of time does not equal hopelessness.

A dear family member of mine was wayward for eight long years. She turned into a very worldly person, almost unrecognizable. She said she would never pray again. She seemed bent on trying every possible vice.

In her own words, "If it made God mad, I did it." I admit I had given up hope of her ever even wanting to return to the Lord, much less going through with it. Shame on me! Circumstances made it necessary for her to have to ask for help. I believe she found that she had ended up in the pigpen. She finally "came to herself" (see Luke 15:17). I will never forget that Sunday morning. As soon as the preacher said "Open your Bibles to Luke 15," tears started streaming down this tired prodigal's face. She went forward during the invitation song, shaking like a leaf. Now, three years later, she is sweeter and stronger than ever.

Of those who shared with me, the time spent away from God ranged from ten months to twenty-five years. Interestingly, the most recurring amount of time was four years. When a loved one falls away, at first we might think, "Surely they'll come back soon. They know better, so they can't have any peace until they make things right." After several months or even a few years, we might conclude they'll never repent. But these interviewed Christians prove there is always hope!

Age is not a factor.

Some fell away as young adults, during their college years. Some fell away as newlyweds. And still some fell away in their middle-aged years. Our faith will be tested in various ways throughout our lives, and each time we will have to decide whether we will "hold fast" (Hebrews 3:6) or let go.

There are wayward among us.

More than one person described themselves as having fallen away even while they continued to attend worship. They were simply going through the motions. Their body was present, but their heart wasn't. Or they were living sinful lifestyles Monday through Saturday. While they fooled others, they knew they were still in the far country. Some explained that only their closest friends and family members knew they weren't right with God. As one brother explained, "I found I could arrive at the last minute and leave right away, so hardly anyone got the opportunity to know me. When I first started drifting away, not many knew.

Sharing my personal life with Christians was inviting involvement I did not want at the time. Few Christians knew much about my life." This is a sobering reminder for us to be involved in the lives of our brothers and sisters in Christ. Let's look around and see who might need extra love and encouragement. I imagine the ones who eventually leave the Lord were once the wayward among us.

Guilt is ever present.

Nearly every participant mentioned guilt. Even if our wayward loved ones look like they no longer care, chances are they are just hiding the fact that they are riddled with guilt.

Reaching out really makes a difference.

As you'll see when you read the responses later in this chapter, the reactions of the wayward to other Christians reaching out to them varied greatly. Some welcomed it; many resented it. But they all remember it. The key is reaching out in the right way, lovingly and humbly.

Becoming wholly committed may take time.

Several explained that while there was a defining moment of wanting to return to the Lord, it took a while for them to "come home" completely. One woman explained that she would still engage in sinful activities occasionally and her heart would bother her. Another said she came forward, but it took her about eight months to get her life straightened out. One gentleman explained his repentance as taking place in phases, a little at a time. Whether they're entangled in an unscriptural relationship or a bad habit, or simply caught up in the world, it may take time for the wayward's heart to be wholly committed once again to God and His will. We must resolve to be patient and understanding when our loved ones struggle to rebuild their faith.

Don't ever give up.

While many of the prodigals rejected those who reached out to them repeatedly, nearly every one advised those with wayward loved ones to never give up. Keep reaching out. Keep trying. One story I heard was about an older gentleman who had been unfaithful for years and years. But then one day a Christian brother simply asked him, "Will I see you in heaven?" A week later the wanderer repented and has been strong and faithful ever since. We just never know what might finally penetrate a wayward heart. Never give up!

In Their Own Words

For the sake of space, I can't include all of the responses, but I selected a few that can be particularly helpful to us. The questions I asked were simple. Their answers were profound.

QUESTION: How did you feel when concerned Christians reached out to you? Did you resent it? Did you feel it was out of love?

My heart was hardened to anything that had to do with God and His people. I didn't want to talk to them. I had no interest in going back. That world had all I "wanted," so I just did not want anything to do with "church." An elder and the preacher came and visited us numerous times. I knew it was out of love, but again, I just did not want anything to do with them. Also, I was embarrassed to be around them as I felt guilty.

I was very uncomfortable. I wanted the conversation to end. BUT ... I never forgot it, and I deeply loved the person for doing it. An elder of the church would take me aside ... tears would fill his eyes. He would tell me he still prayed often for my whole family and that he missed us at church and worried very much about our souls. I never resented it. I felt like he was a true Christian. I longed to be right with God, but wasn't entirely ready yet. To this day [my husband] and I have searched for him to let him know how he impacted my life. We have not been able to find him, but we know that someday he will know.

Sadly, I don't remember anyone ever trying to reach out to me in those very lonely years.

I didn't really like it when Christians came to visit because it made me feel guilty. But I'm glad they did because it was a reminder of what I should be doing and that I could come back.

I can honestly say that I never resented when people tried to reach out to me. First, I knew it was a task of the church body as a whole, if not the elders. Did I know it was out of love? Yes, in my heart I think I did. But at the time, I think I was more focused on the fact that it was just a duty. Regardless, I knew they were doing their "job," and the fact was I wasn't doing my "job."

It depended on the person. When people who I felt didn't really know me reached out, it made me really angry. I felt like what I did was none of their business, especially if the only time I had spoken to them was when they were "condemning" me. I felt their attempts were mostly made from their desire to let me know how "Christian" they were and how "un-Christian" I was.

I rationalized that they were judging me and I resented it terribly. I felt it was not out of love, but perhaps [out of] not really understanding the things in my life I was going through, and probably if they were in my position they would be making the same bad choices I had made. Looking back I realize the true Christians were the ones who really cared about my soul and were bold enough to speak up and make me accountable for my mistakes.

The close Christian friends I had were concerned, of course. I was good at letting them know I would try harder. When they said God loves me, I would say thank you, and agree, but inside I felt pity for their ignorance in the belief of a higher power. I felt I could be a good moral person without God. In fact, I believed that not having God made me a better person because then I wouldn't be like "all" the Christians I knew and judge people based on what the Bible says.

I wish more people had been willing to talk to me. Only two people ever approached me, and one of those people was my own mother. And they were very short conversations, maybe two or three minutes. I've managed some people at work for quite some time now and it's odd, but there are a lot of similarities between having a performance improvement conversation with someone you manage and reaching out to a fellow Christian going through a difficult time. The conversation is uncomfortable. No one enjoys talking about difficult things. No one enjoys being told they are not meeting expectations. Even when the conversation is in the kindest, most loving way, the person on the receiving end feels uncomfortable and realizes they are not meeting expectations. It's uncertain, even scary—you never know how the person on the receiving end is going to react. But regardless, the conversation is absolutely necessary. In one instance, a person's job depends on having the conversation. Much more importantly, in the other instance, a person's soul depends on having the conversation.

At first I blew them off, and then I felt aggravated. I felt like, "Who are they to judge me?" They didn't know what I was going through. (No one knew.) I felt I was a number, not a member, that the church wanted back high numbers and wasn't really concerned with me personally.

QUESTION: What made you decide to come back?

One day a man came to the place where I worked and quoted Scripture and it hit me that God was missing from my life. I looked up the local congregation and we went the following Sunday. The congregation welcomed us in as if they had been waiting for us all of their lives. From then on we grew exponentially in the Lord and here we are!

I came back to the church after finding out I was pregnant. My fiancé and I went forward at church, mostly because my dad was the preacher and I knew it was expected. Their response to our public admission of sin was incredible. It was a game changer for me because I was preparing to make my absence from the church permanent. (I assumed people would react badly and was angry in advance.) Instead, I was so overwhelmed by the outpouring of love that I couldn't help but stick around.

I came back when I went through an extremely trying time in my life and I received so much love and support from my spiritual family. There was nothing I could do to fix the situation but rely on God.

It has taken heartbreaking major events to wake me up, but I am here to stay.

I think I had reached the lowest point in my life. Everything was lost. What brought me back to God was knowing in my heart how much I had hurt the ones I love. I knew God's arms were open and ready for me to come home.

It wasn't until my world felt like it was falling apart that I consciously turned to God. Eventually ... I felt hope spring into my heart, I felt I was loved and understood fully, and I felt there was actually a purpose for my existence.

I guess I finally decided to come back when I would see my son getting older and I didn't want him growing up and not knowing God. I knew if my relationship wasn't right with God then my son's wouldn't be either. [My husband and I] both decided it was time to get it right. My thing was I never forgot about God. I was always thinking about Him and what He wanted from me. I just didn't want to listen. I'm so thankful to have come to my senses and returned to Him, and I'm so thankful for His forgiveness.

I hated to live a double life, and that is what I felt like I was doing. I had to learn to love myself a small portion of how much God loves me. I know it sounds trite, but it was a very big deal for me at the time!

A loving and persistent friend. An elder's wife visited regularly and was very blunt, but genuinely concerned. She didn't know the full extent of my sin and never asked. She saw me torn up at my worst, hurting, helpless, and hopeless. She helped me get healthy. She never candy-coated anything and wasn't afraid of the resistance I kept giving. She cried with me, studied with me, and showed me I was needed, but that I had to completely stop the continual sin, repent, and start being an active part of the church.

If I'm truly honest with myself, my children are what brought me all the way back. Realizing that God has given us these two little girls who will one day grow up into young women is an overwhelming responsibility. And if there is one thing I learned from my own upbringing, it is that any hypocrisy from a parent, from one in a position of authority, will only lead to confusion. So I do my best to give them a consistent environment—one where they don't feel like they need to act differently when they are with their church family or others. My hope is that they only act in one way, as a Christian, as they were raised to be.

QUESTION: What advice would you give someone who has a loved one who has fallen away?

Be very patient. It takes some people longer to realize where they are. Always be there and don't ever give up on them. Perhaps it will be the 105th time they finally listen. Let them know you want what is best for their eternal salvation.

Christians may feel they haven't done any good because the wayward didn't do anything right away, but the wayward will remember all the cards and visits and prayers. I remember all the cards I got. I wasn't ready emotionally then, but God gave me time.

Continue to pray. God is listening even if you don't think your loved one is. He will never force their heart to change, but He will always continue to touch their lives in ways you cannot. Occasionally let them know you care and miss them. I think we all have a responsibility to let those we love know that how they are living is putting them in danger of losing their salvation, without doing it so often that we alienate them. Don't give them the illusion that you think they are safe. You will regret that. I have had to crawl out of that hole myself with extended family. It is harder to be completely honest with someone that you have wanted to protect their feelings for years, than it would be if you had lovingly handled [it] from the beginning.

It's a fine line to walk between acceptance of sin and acceptance of a sinner, but support them when and where you can. I think sometimes we get caught up in publicly shaming people who are living in sin, and we forget that for the most part they are already ashamed. I remember how difficult it was to sleep sometimes because of the guilt, but to be honest the guilt was easier to deal with than the fear of confessing my sin to people and wondering how they would react ...

Study with them where they are spiritually. I had been a Christian for several years, but didn't know anything.

Love, listen, and patience. A person who has someone close to them fall away from the Lord must continue to love the one who has fallen away. It will hurt the faithful one so much. They will feel powerless and fear for the one who has fallen away. But it will mean more than words can say to the one who has fallen away. To know that no matter what you have done you are still loved means there is hope. There is hope for you. There is hope for your soul. There is hope for you to overcome whatever has separated you from God. Pray that you can be patient, that their heart will be opened, that you can find the right words when the opportunity presents itself, and that God's will be done.

Don't think you can fix their problems without God's help. Believe in prayer. Part of James 5:16 reads, "The prayers of a righteous man avails much." This indicates to me that if I want my prayers to be well heard, I need to be as righteous as I can be. And in prayer, don't try to tell God what you think needs to be done. Be willing to turn it over to Him and understand only He can help. Ask yourself, "What if I were no longer here? Who has the only real power to help?" Pray that God will do what's best for their soul.

Put God first in all things, and be the best example of a righteous person you can be. Try to be an example in every phone call, every Facebook post, and in every visit. When they share issues with you, try to be prepared through your study of God's Word to respond with scriptural references.

Pray, pray, pray! Unless you know them very well, don't just assume that because they have always "gone to church" they know what the Bible says. We never know what goes on in a home unless we live in that home. There may be dysfunctions of which we are not aware, and the one who has fallen away may have confusions, frustrations, anger, or other things blocking their way to God that patient teaching may help clear away.

Additional Thoughts

I often think of Proverbs 22:6: 'Train up a child in the way he should go, and when he is old he will not depart from it." In many ways, we are all children before we come to the

Lord, and this verse gives me hope that if a person was able to accept the Lord once, then the knowledge is there for them to open their hearts and accept Him again. That's hope straight from the pages of God's Word, and it doesn't get much better than that.

The worst part of being wayward and coming back is forgiving yourself or the pain you caused the ones you love. There are scars from being in the far country. We do reap what we sow.

It has been a long road back, but each and every day I feel better about my relationship with God, and I see more and more of His light in my life. I realize how truly important it is to surround yourself with your Christian family. Surrounding yourself with all the good influences you can helps keep the evil influences at bay.

I knew that my choices and actions were willful sins on my behalf. Looking back, it was not an issue of belief. It was an issue of obedience. I knew what I needed to do with my life. I simply chose not to do it. I chose to be in the world.

I have lots of regret. I realize how much my choices in life affected the lives of those around me, those I loved most. I was seeing a trickle-down effect. My son is struggling with life and relationships ... my grandchildren are being raised without the teachings of Christ in their daily lives .... Today I see how [my son's] life and those of my grandchildren have been affected. They have been cheated by my actions. Although I have all this regret, I view the future as a way to make a difference in my loved ones' lives and all who know me today. I think of Saul/Paul. Certainly he regretted the pain he caused before his conversion, but he spent the rest of his life in dedicated service to our Lord.

∽Faith in Action∼

Contact someone you know who used to be wayward. Tell them you appreciate their courage and conviction and that their example of returning to the Lord offers you hope for your own wayward loved ones.

Apply Your Heart (Proverbs 2:2)

1. Read Luke 15:11–32. Circle each time you see the word "father." What do you learn about our Father from this text?

2. Relationship is key to reaching out to the wayward. How can we develop deeper relationships with those in our congregation who seem to want to keep things superficial?

3. When asked the reason for their return, former wayward members gave different answers. What seem to be the most common reasons? How does this information help us as we consider our own wayward loved ones?

4. What reasons were given for the resentment the wayward felt toward the "interference" of concerned Christians? What motives did wayward members attribute to other Christians?

5. What specific things can we say and do to ensure that the wayward know we love them and that our concern is genuine?

6. Perhaps the most difficult challenge is knowing how to demonstrate constant love without seeming to condone a sinful lifestyle, especially if the wayward is a close family member. How can we express our love without offering false peace? What are the dangers of pretending like everything is okay?

An Elder's Perspective

For this last perspective, I wanted to ask an elder some questions about wayward members in general. Mark Hanstein is an elder at the Bear Valley Church of Christ in Denver, Colorado. I chose him because I have seen him reach out to wayward members. He has a tender heart, a knowledge of God's Word, and a "Think Souls" mentality.

QUESTION: What scriptures do you rely on as you reach out to wayward members?

As this relates to me, I am reminded of Luke 19:10—that Jesus has come to seek and to save that which was lost. I am also reminded of 2 Corinthians 5:10 and 11. As I recall, the older versions (KJV and ASV I think) translate 11 as "knowing the terror of the Lord, we persuade men." I know what the judgment holds for the unprepared and thus try to persuade others. Later Paul speaks of the ministry of reconciliation (v. 18) and the word of reconciliation (v. 19). Then he speaks of the idea of being "ambassadors for Christ." Then he says, "as though God were making an appeal through us" to be reconciled to Christ (v. 20 [NASB]). Galatians 6:1 refers to the fact that the "spiritual" (hopefully elders are that) must restore, in a spirit of gentleness, those overtaken in any trespass. First Thessalonians 5:14 tells church leaders to admonish, encourage, and help those who struggle spiritually (see also 2 Thessalonians 3:15). The task of keeping watch over souls is mentioned in Hebrews 13:17. James 5:19, 20 speaks of turning sinners back from the error of their way, thus saving a soul from death and covering a multitude of sins. Jude 22, 23 speaks of having mercy on some and snatching others out of the fire. These are just a few of the Scriptures that motivate me to reach out to wayward members. These passages remind me of my obligation as a Christian to others as well as remind me of my responsibility as an elder to others.

QUESTION: How do you approach them? What do you say?

As this relates to wayward members, I tell them that I want to talk to them about their soul. I mention that I am concerned about whatever the problem in their life is (lack of attendance, other issues). I try to remind them of the fact that at one time be-ing forgiven of their sins and in a right relationship with God was important to them and should be now. I have asked them, why else were you baptized if not for these reasons (I know avoiding hell is another, but I try to emphasize the other two things here). I also ask what contributed to the current state of affairs (waywardness) in their life. I often hear how the church in some way let them down, or of some kind of hypocrisy among members, or of being forced to go to church as a child, or of anger to-ward someone. Some will speak of trying to resolve their spiritual struggles or upside down life by themselves. I encourage them to let us help them and inform them that we are already praying for them. I remind them that we are not perfect and we would be willing to make right whatever is wrong. With many I remind them of the certain return of Christ and the need to be prepared for it by living a life in anticipation of it (Ecclesiastes 12:13, 14; Luke 12:35–40; Acts 17:30, 31; 1 Thessalonians 5:1–10). I don't quit early or give up easily on these people (in spite of the fact that I may start this process late with several) as I am pushing toward a definite resolution of the matter of their spiritual life. I do try to do this with directness and gentleness and humility. I al-ways offer to study with them, any time, any place. I always try to do these things face to face, not by phone, email, or text. That's just my personal preference, but among other things it gives me a chance to size them up and gauge the situation.

QUESTION: What advice would you give someone who has a loved one who has fallen away?

In a case of disfellowship, I remind people that God's way is the best way, the right way, and works to bring about the repentance of the wayward. I encourage them to respect this, act accordingly, and do nothing to undermine the intent of a legitimate action of church discipline/disfellowship. I inform them that the disfellowshipped per-son needs to feel that he has lost something precious as long as his current spiritual state exists. Thus, as hard as it is to do, a family needs to close ranks on this and abide by the Lord's will in order for the sinner to feel the need to repent. To do otherwise would actually encourage the sinner to maintain his lost/wayward path and under-mine the effort to restore him. This same framework applies to Christian brethren/ friends who may be reluctant to take a hard line with someone they love, though wayward (and lost).

In cases where the wayward/fallen away have not been disfellowshipped, I sometimes find family members inclined to defend the position of the wayward and see me (or the church) as an adversary of some kind. In those situations, I try and persuade them to work with me to bring the wayward back to faithfulness. This can be slow going, so I try to make sure the door is always left open for additional conversations to this end.

In cases where the faithful family member and the wayward are not on the best of terms, I encourage them to pray for the wayward and remind them that God in His providence can bring about a good end to this matter (for example, Philemon and Onesimus). I remind them to be the best example they can be, because their life will say more than their words ever will (1 Peter 3:1–6; Matthew 5:13–16). I encourage the family member to make whatever apologies and amends are necessary in an effort to make things right with the wayward. I also encourage the family member to tell (or write) the wayward that they love them, are concerned for their soul and why, will do anything to help them spiritually, and are praying specifically for them. I use this same basic framework in encouraging family members who are still on good terms with the wayward, as well.

I remind people of the passages that motivate me (see answer to question one) and suggest that they not lose heart in their efforts to bring about the repentance of another. I also remind them of the need to be patient as matters like these tend to take time. I stress that they need to maintain their own faithfulness to God and His word. I also tell them that as long as there is time, there is hope for their wayward loved one. I also offer to do whatever I can to help in the matter.

Appendix

Bible-Marking Exercises

B ible marking is a method of Bible study that encourages the reader to follow a chain of scriptures on a single topic to get a cohesive picture of the topic being studied. It is especially helpful to gain a broader understanding of how scriptures fit together. The reader follows the path of verses from its beginning point to reach a logical conclusion, underlining and highlighting texts as she goes.

Backsliding: A Bible-Marking Exercise

If you take a few minutes to mark this topic in your Bible, you will always be prepared to study with someone who believes in "once saved, always saved." You'll be able to help your wayward loved ones see how God feels about those who turn away from Him.

Faithfulness is a lifelong, intentional choice. Over and over in the Scriptures, God warned His people against backsliding. He used terms like "falling away," "forgetting," "departing," "rejecting," and "turning back." Pay special attention to God's reaction and what He warned would happen to those who backslid. In the front of your Bible, write "Backsliding—Deuteronomy 4:1-10."

Hold Fast

In context, Moses was telling the people that God had rules for them to follow so they would know how to live in the land they were about to possess. In verse 1, underline "listen to the statutes and the judgments which I teach you to observe, that you may live." In verses 3-4, Moses reminded them that God destroyed those who turned away from Him. Underline verse 4 and circle "held fast." Then underline verse 9 and circle the words "forget" and "depart." At the end of verse 10, write 29:10-20.

Underline "covenant with the LORD" in verse 12. Underline "a people for Himself" in verse 13. In verse 18, underline "so that there may not be among you man or woman or family or tribe, whose heart turns away today from the LORD our God" and circle "turns away." Underline the special warning found in verse 19 and the consequences in verse 20. At the end of verse 20, write 1 Samuel 15:10-26.

Obey the Lord

In this passage, Samuel was confronting Saul for not obeying God. Saul started out strong, but instead of growing in his faith, he ended up rejecting God. Draw a squiggly line under "turned back" in verse 11. (Notice how not only God but those who love us grieve when we turn away from the Lord.)

In verse 13, underline "I have performed the commandment of the
LORD" and, in the margin, write "partial obedience = disobedience." Underline Samuel's question in verse 19, "Why then did you not obey the
voice of the LORD?", and Saul's reply in verse 20, "But I have obeyed the
voice of the LORD." Notice that some form of the word "obey" is used five
times in verses 19-22. (The word "heed/listen" at the end of verse 22 is the
same word as "obey" in the original language.) Circle the words "rebellion," "stubbornness," and "rejected" in verse 23 and underline "Because
you have rejected the word of the LORD, He also has rejected you from
being king." Underline it again in verse 26. At the end of verse 26, write
I Kings 11:1-11.

King Solomon ended up turning his heart away from God. In verse 3,
underline "turned away his heart." In verse 4, underline "his heart was
not loyal to the LORD his God." In verse 6, underline "did evil in the sight
of the LORD, and did not fully follow the LORD." In verse 9, underline "his
heart had turned from the LORD God." And then in verse 11, underline
his sad outcome: "Because you have done this, and have not kept My
covenant and My statutes, which I have commanded you, I will surely
tear the kingdom away from you." At the end of verse 11, write Psalm 85:8.

Turn Back

» Underline "let them not turn back to folly" and put a square
   around "turn back." At the end of the verse, write Jeremiah 2:19.
» Underline the words "backslidings" and "forsaken." At the end of
   the verse, write 3:6-22.
» Underline each occurrence of the word "backsliding" (vv. 6, 8, 11,
   12, 14, and twice in 22). Circle each occurrence of the word "return"
   (vv. 7, 12, 14, and 22). Draw squiggly lines under "but she did not
   return" in verse 7, "iniquity" in verse 13, "transgressed" in verse 13,
   "turn away" in verse 19, and "forgotten" in verse 21. At the end of
   verse 22, write Ezekiel 3:20, 21.
» Underline "when a righteous man turns from his righteousness."
   At the end of verse 21, write 33:18.

» Underline the entire verse. At the end, write Luke 9:62.

» Underline "looking back" and, in the margin, write "Farmers know you can't plow a straight row looking backward." At the end of the verse, write Galatians 1:6.

» Underline "turning away" and, at the end of the verse, write 1 Timothy 1:19.

» Underline "concerning the faith have suffered shipwreck" and, at the end of the verse, write 6:10.

» Underline "strayed from the faith" and, at the end of the verse, write Hebrews 3:12-14.

» Draw a squiggly line under "departing from the living God" and "hardened through the deceitfulness of sin." Underline all of verse 14 and circle the word "if." At the end of the verse, write 10:26, 27.

» Underline "sin willfully after we have received the knowledge of truth" in verse 26 and the words "judgment" and "fiery indignation" in verse 27. At the end of the verse, write vv. 38, 39.

» Underline "draws back" in verse 38 and "draw back" in verse 39. At the end of the verse, write 2 Peter 2:20, 21.

» Circle "again entangled" in verse 20 and "to turn" in verse 21. Underline "the latter end is worse for them than the beginning" in verse 20. At the end of verse 21, write Revelation 2:4, 5.

» Underline "you have left your first love" in verse 4. Put a square around the solution in verse 5: "remember" and "repent."

Sinful Past: A Bible-Marking Exercise

When wayward loved ones return to the Lord, they are really beginning a whole new and sometimes painful journey. They may struggle with guilt. They may feel unworthy to serve in various ways in the church. It may take a while for them to feel whole again. If you mark this topic in your Bible, you will be able to show them some passages that will help them move past their guilt.

Of all the topics I've marked, this is in the top three of ones I refer to most often. So many people struggle with things in their past. Guilt consumes those who have made dreadful decisions or hurt loved ones. Some feel as if their sin is too big for God's grace. Some think that acting like a good Christian now when they were so different in the past is the same as playing the hypocrite. The purpose of this topic is to be able to see what God can do for those who struggle with a sinful past. In the front of your Bible, write "Sinful Past—Luke 7:36-50."

Your Sins Are Forgiven

In verse 37, circle "a sinner." In the margin next to it, write "bad reputation." The word "sinner" was used for those who were known to be immoral. Most likely, this woman was a prostitute. At the end of verse 39, circle "a sinner" and underline "who and what manner of woman this is who is touching Him, for she is a sinner." In the margin next to it, write "how others viewed her." In verse 47, circle "her sins" and underline "which are many." Squiggly underline "are forgiven." In verse 48, circle "Your sins" and squiggly underline "are forgiven." Jesus had just referred to her "many" sins, but now they are ALL forgiven. In verse 50, squiggly underline, "Your faith has saved you. Go in peace."

Do you think she would've struggled with her sinful past? We know she had a tender heart, as evidenced by her tears. Jesus offered comfort. He wanted her to know she could live in peace from now on. He extolled her virtues (vv. 44-46) and made it clear she was every bit as righteous now as the religious leader (and actually more so). In the margin next to verse 50, write "comfort & assurance!" At the end of verse 50, write Acts 2:36-38.

A Crucified Flesh

In verse 36, underline "whom you crucified." In verse 38, underline "for the remission of sins." What were these people guilty of? See verse 36. What could have been more dreadful than that? And yet, they were offered complete forgiveness of their sins and the gift of the Holy Spirit. At the end of verse 38, write Galatians 5:19-24.

In verse 19, squiggly underline "works of the flesh." In verse 24, squiggly underline "crucified the flesh" and draw a line connecting the phrase "works of the flesh" in verse 19 down to "crucified the flesh" in verse 24. Underline all of verse 24. Those who belong to Jesus are able to put to death the fleshly activities of a former lifestyle. At the end of verse 24, write Colossians 2:12, 13.

In verse 13, underline "dead in your trespasses." What are "trespasses"? In the margin, write "breaking a command." In verse 13, underline "having forgiven you all trespasses." Which trespasses are forgiven? Circle the word "all." Do you see a contrast in verse 13? Draw a square around the words "dead" and "alive." At the end of verse 13, write 1 Timothy 1:12-16.

Abundant Grace

In verse 13, squiggly underline "although I was formerly a blasphemer, a persecutor, and an insolent man." Notice Paul's past: (1) "blasphemer"—one who violates the glory of God, one who mocks the power of God; (2) "persecutor"—read Acts 8:3, 4; 22:4, 5, 19; and (3) "insolent man"—although two words in our English text, this comes from one Greek word (hybristes).

This word is found only one other time in the New Testament (Romans 1:30). Read Romans 1:28-32. In verse 30, the word is translated "violent" and found in the middle of a list of things that are "undiscerning," "untrustworthy," "unloving," and "deserving of death." In 1 Timothy 1:15, squiggly underline "sinners, of whom I am chief." Circle the beautiful words for those who are now in Christ: "mercy" (v. 13); "grace," "faith," and "love" (v. 14); and "all longsuffering" (v. 16).

In verse 14, how was grace described? As adequate? No. Underline "exceedingly abundant." In verse 12, underline the three things Paul said Christ did for him: (1) "enabled me"; (2) "counted me faithful"; and (3) "putting me into the ministry." (I wrote a little 1, 2, and 3 next to each of those in my Bible.) Consider each of those things. How are they significant to one who struggles with a sinful past? At the end of verse 16, write 1 Corinthians 6:9-11.

Cleansed from All Sin

In verse 9, underline "the unrighteous." In verse 11, squiggly underline "such were some of you." Members of the church at Corinth had been guilty of adultery, homosexuality, drunkenness, theft, etc. In verse 11, circle the three things that gave those Christians a clean slate: "washed," "sanctified," and "justified" (you can write in the margin "'just-as-if-I'd' never sinned"). At the end of verse 11, write 1 John 1:7-9.

In verse 7, circle "if" and squiggly underline "we walk in the light." Underline "the blood of Jesus Christ His Son cleanses us from all sin." Which sins? Put a square around "all." In verse 9, circle "if" and squiggly underline "we confess our sins." Underline "He is faithful and just to forgive us our sins and to cleanse us from all unrighteousness." Which unrighteous acts? Put a square around "all."

Those who struggle with a sinful past can be consumed with guilt. It can prevent them from serving to their fullest potential. It can keep them from experiencing the joy that comes from being in Christ. One important question must be asked: *who* wants Christians to feel that way? As we've seen from the Scriptures we've looked at, it clearly isn't our Lord. He makes it possible for us to leave our past behind and embrace the grace He offers. Satan wants us to be bound to our past. But like Paul, we can be used by God in big ways through His mercy and for His glory!

Grace: A Bible-Marking Exercise

Grace can be misunderstood in at least a couple of different ways. Some abuse grace by using it to justify their unscriptural marriage or other sin. They'll say, "God's grace covers it." Some go to the other extreme and feel there's not enough grace to cover their sin. They believe they've gone too far to deserve God's grace. Both of these viewpoints are dangerous for the wayward. If you mark this topic in your Bible, you will be prepared to help others understand the accurate, biblical view of grace.

"Grace to you and peace from God our Father and the Lord Jesus Christ" (Romans 1:7). This phrase is found in every single letter Paul wrote. Paul embraced God's grace and found it important to write about. It's a key word in his letter to the Romans, appearing at least twenty-four times. Even though "grace" is a common word in the Bible, it's commonly misunderstood. It's important that our understanding of grace be based on what God has to say. In the front of your Bible, write "Grace—Romans 5:1, 2."

Let Grace Reign

» Underline "justified by faith" and circle the word "peace" in verse 1. Underline "access by faith" and circle the word "grace" in verse 2. Then draw a square around "Lord Jesus Christ," who makes both peace and grace possible. At the end of verse 2, write v. 17.

» Circle "abundance of grace." Draw a squiggly line under "reign in life." Underline "through ... Jesus Christ." This beautiful verse shows the contrast between sin and grace. Sin allowed death to reign, but the grace of Jesus allows all who are in Him to reign in life. I love the word "abundance." There's enough grace to cover any past! At the end of the verse, write v. 21.

» Circle "grace" and underline "reign through righteousness" and "through Jesus Christ." Grace can reign in our lives as long as we're striving to live righteously. At the end of the verse, write Acts 20:32.

» Circle "grace" and underline "able to build you up" and "give you an inheritance." Draw a squiggly line under "all those who are sanctified." Notice that each of these passages so far has indicated that grace is for those who are in Christ, living righteously, sanctified, etc. At the end of the verse, write 2 Corinthians 4:15.

» Circle "grace" and underline "cause thanksgiving to abound." Just as grace is abundant, our thanksgiving for it should be abundant. At the end of the verse, write Ephesians 2:5.

What Grace Can Do for You

» Circle "grace" and underline "you have been saved." Grace saves! At the end of the verse, write 2 Thessalonians 2:16.

» Circle "grace" and underline "everlasting consolation and good hope." Grace brings consolation and hope! At the end of the verse, write 2 Timothy 2:1.

» Circle "grace" and underline "be strong" and "in Christ Jesus." Grace strengthens! At the end of the verse, write Titus 2:11.

» Circle "grace" and underline "brings salvation" and "all men." Saving grace is offered to all! At the end of the verse, write Galatians 1:6.

What You Can Do with Grace

» Circle "grace" and underline "turning away." Grace can be rejected. At the end of the verse, write 5:4.

» Circle "grace" and underline "you have fallen from" and "estranged from Christ." One CAN fall from grace. At the end of the verse, write 1 Timothy 1:14.

» Circle "grace" and underline "exceedingly abundant" and "in Christ Jesus." In context, Paul was writing about his sinful past (see vv. 13, 15). He was thankful for the generous measure of God's grace. At the end of the verse, write Jude 4.

» Circle "grace" and underline "turn ... into lewdness." Lewdness involves indulgence and immorality. Some may claim that God's grace covers their sinful lifestyle, but this verse teaches that grace can be abused and misused. Remember, grace is for those who are striving to live righteously. At the end of the verse, write Romans 6:1, 2.

» Circle "grace" and underline the entire passage. At the end of the verse, write vv. 15-18.
» Circle "grace" and underline verses 15 and 18.

These are just a few of the many passages about grace. It would be a great personal Bible study to look up all of them and see what else you can learn. May God's grace reign in all of our lives!